Siblings and sociology

Manchester University Press

Siblings and sociology

Katherine Davies

MANCHESTER UNIVERSITY PRESS

Published by Manchester University Press
Oxford Road, Manchester M13 9PL

www.manchesteruniversitypress.co.uk

British Library Cataloguing-in-Publication Data
A catalogue record for this book is available from the British Library

ISBN   978 1 5261 4217 7   hardback

First published 2023

Typeset
by New Best-set Typesetters Ltd

For Rory and Ewan

Contents

Acknowledgements

First, I would like to thank the young people who participated in focus groups and interviews and the mass observers who responded to a directive on sibling relationships. The insights of these participants form the basis for much of this book. Bringing together these rich datasets has been a hugely rewarding and illuminating endeavour. The Mass Observation Project material is reproduced by permission of Curtis Brown Group Ltd, London, on behalf of The Trustees of the Mass Observation Archive © The Trustees of the Mass Observation Archive.

I would also like to thank the Morgan Centre for the Study of Everyday Life which funded the Mass Observation Project directive used in parts of this book and which, more importantly, provided the intellectual home where many of the ideas discussed here were first sparked. In particular I am grateful to Wendy Bottero for her encouragement and advice, and to Jennifer Mason whose work and mentorship has helped inspire much of my writing on siblings.

I am very grateful to my friends and colleagues in Sociological Studies at the University of Sheffield, particularly Sarah Neal and Lauren White who so kindly read drafts and provided invaluable feedback. Also thank you to Nathan Hughes for helping me to carve out space to work on the book, to Jo Britton and Kate Reed for their encouragement and positivity during our lockdown 'book club', to Laura Towers for sharing my fascination with siblings, and to Matthias Benzer for his friendship and support. I am also grateful to my other academic friends for their kindness and patience in listening to my worries and ramblings about the progress of the book, especially Gemma Edwards and Helene Snee.

Artist Ruth Palmer was incredibly generous in granting permission for me to use her beautiful painting *Deep Roots* for the cover of this book. The painting perfectly sums up the themes of siblings growing up as individuals with intertwined biographies which I explore in this volume. Ruth's work can be found on her website: www.ruthpalmerfineart.com.

It was very hard to write this book and there were many times, particularly during COVID-19 lockdowns, when the pressures of home schooling and online teaching felt insurmountable. I am grateful to my mum and dad, Margaret and Philip Davies, and my sister Lizzy who all helped with childcare whenever they could. Most of all I am eternally grateful to my partner Sean, who supported me in so many ways and did everything he could to help me find the time to keep writing. I would never have finished without his help. Finally I am thankful to my children Rory and Ewan, whose sibling relationship continues to be an inspiration.

Some of the chapters in the book contain revised and adapted extracts from the following articles: K. Davies, 'Siblings, Stories and the Self: The Sociological Significance of Young People's Sibling Relationships', *Sociology* 49.4 (2015), 679–95; K. Davies, '"Sticky" Proximities: Sibling Relationships and Education', *The Sociological Review* 67.1 (2019), 210–25.

Introduction: why siblings matter

The importance of siblings

Writing about siblings in the midst of the 2020–21 COVID-19 global pandemic has meant both that this book is very late and that the experience of writing it has been imbued with sibling relationships in ways I could not have imagined. Schools and nurseries in the UK first closed as part of a national lockdown in March 2020, and my 7- and 4-year-old children were at home full time. Their relationship intensified as they became each other's only playmates, and the complexities and contradictions of being and having a sibling were amplified. In any one day their relationship might have included frayed tempers, elaborate imaginative shared games, laughter, tears, play fights, real fights, care, companionship and, of course, boredom and irritation. News outlets published stories about increased loneliness among only children during this period, with headlines such as 'Coronavirus: Is Lockdown Making Only Children Lonely?' (Griffiths, 2020) used by the BBC in April 2020 – and there was a sense that children and their siblings were lucky to 'have one another'.

My partner and I tried our best to be fair in the ways we parented our two children, but sometimes struggled to make things 'equal'. During the first school closure, our older son had to complete school work at home on most days while our youngest – still at nursery – did not. There was also a period of a few months when nurseries reopened, but our older child's school year was not included in the UK government's first wave of returns, and the prospect of only one of them being able to go back out into the world was difficult to navigate. Other sibling relationships also came to the fore during this time. At one point, with older relatives all isolating, I phoned my sister to ask for help with childcare. She caught the train to visit us as soon as there was a loosening in lockdown rules, a favour that felt too great to ask of anyone else. Anxious about the health of his parents, my partner keenly felt the loss of his only sibling, who had died two years previously, imagining how they might have worked together to support their mum and dad at such a worrying time.

These sorts of experiences are not rare, and many families in the UK and beyond will have faced similar or much greater challenges during the pandemic; we were very fortunate to be healthy and to have jobs and a safe and pleasant home. However, this account of life in the UK during the 2020–21 coronavirus lockdowns does highlight the significance of sibling relationships. The complexities and contradictions of sibling relationships were brought to the fore, and the ways in which siblingship can be characterised simultaneously by companionship and conflict and, particularly for children sharing a home, a sensorial and embodied proximity became clear. Moralities, norms and stereotypes about the benefits that ought to be derived from children's sibling relationships were also prevalent, and the anxieties expressed in the media about the welfare of children with no siblings at this time reflect wider assumptions about the importance of growing up alongside siblings and the significance of lateral relationships and generational proximity for children's development.

Similarly, the responsibility felt by parents to be 'fair' highlights the centrality of equality to normative assumptions about how siblingship ought to be done and how siblings should be treated. This again points to something of a paradox: siblings must be treated as individuals – their different home-schooling requirements and unique needs must be acknowledged and accommodated – yet they are also part of a sibling group (a sibship) and as such must be treated with a degree of sameness, the implication being that failure to do so will unleash negative emotions commonly associated with sibling relationships, such as jealousy. The example of siblingship in lockdown also indicates how – even when growing up together, close in age and in a similar home environment – siblings can experience wider socio-economic or macropolitical events differently in ways that challenge the ideal of equality (reflected in my family's experience of the children having different access to education, with only one child able to return 'early' to a formal educational setting and only one child having to learn from home).

In this reflection on my own experience, we also see how siblings continue to be important beyond childhood. Though adult sibling relationships might be characterised by greater geographical distance and less regular contact, they can often continue to be a source of care and support which can be activated when needed. It is revealing that the help provided by my sister during lockdown was not something I could have asked of anyone else, such as a friend or more distant family member. The lateral nature of the tie with my sister, who is a similar age to me, meant she was not as vulnerable to COVID-19 as my parents, and the fact that we are related meant that my sister had connections to my children (as their aunt) and my partner (as his sister-in-law) and as such probably felt some degree of obligation to help (Finch and Mason, 1993). Sibling relationships might ebb and flow through the life course and there are often certain moments, such as when parents require care, when these relationships take on a renewed significance; we saw this in my partner's experiences of missing his late sister at this time.

These themes point to the significance of sibling relationships in people's lives. They are also deeply sociological and pertain to issues that are central to the discipline: relationships, care, morality, normativity, identity and life course as well as emotions. It is surprising, then, that despite a small but growing body of rich empirical work examining sibling relationships, work on siblingship has not infiltrated sociological thought more generally. The role of lateral relationships with siblings has often been overlooked in the framing and explaining of social processes such as the formation of the social self, the relational construction of identity, the inculcation of cultural and social capital, experiences of institutions such as school and the influence of being and having siblings on people's life course transitions. The focus instead has been predominantly on parent–child relationships and the role of adults in shaping the lives of children and young people. This book brings siblings to the fore by exploring the sociological significance of sibling relationships in two key ways. First, it will demonstrate why and how siblings matter, both in our lives but also in wider processes that have occupied sociological thought such as those pertaining to the self, relationality, imagination and normativity, as well as temporality and the life course. Secondly, the book asks what sociological insights can be gained by using sibling relationships as a lens through which to re-examine these central sociological ideas and think about them in different ways. As such, it considers how we can think sociologically about siblings, outlining some of the key ways that sibling relationships are sociologically significant, as well as exploring how using sibling relationships as a lens to think with can contribute to sociological thought.

Siblings are intriguing

Despite often being on the periphery of sociological thinking, siblings carry a certain public fascination. Siblings are often depicted in novels, films and television series in ways that emphasise the significance of the relational form in people's lives, as well as pointing to features of siblingship which seem particularly intriguing (Stephens Mink and Doubler Ward, 1993) such as the idea that sibling relationships are imbued with emotion. Disney's 2013 hit film *Frozen*, for instance, revolves around the relationship between two sisters, the big plot twist being that the act of 'true love' on which the story pivots is one of sisterly, rather than romantic, love. The idea of a special bond between siblings is also often used as a central feature in stories of 'long-lost' siblings, who discover resemblances or find that their relatedness explains an uncanny bond. These tropes of long-lost siblingship are often the basis of popular 'real life' family reunion shows and are evident in fictional portrayals such as the characters Luke and Leia in the original *Star Wars* trilogy, who, discovering they are brother and sister, realise that they both possess The Force and a certain sort of extrasensory perception. Jealousy and rivalry are also often used as central plot devices, with the deadly rivalry between the Old Testament brothers Cain and Abel being the basis for many depictions of sibling jealousy (particularly between brothers). Examples include John Steinbeck's 1952 novel *East of Eden*, which is based on the Cain and Abel story, and the rivalry between three brothers in the mafia family at the heart of the 1972 film *The Godfather*. Relationships between step-siblings are also often depicted as being characterised by heightened conflict and jealousy, the most obvious example being the 'ugly sisters' in the classic fairy tale 'Cinderella', where a lack of resemblance between the beautiful Cinderella and her ugly step-sisters is used to emphasise other differences between them. Probing and scrutinising ideas of similarity and difference between siblings creates beguiling characters and facilitates the telling of captivating stories. For example, siblings with different personality traits are a key feature of a number of Jane Austen's novels – the Bennett sisters in *Pride and Prejudice*, for instance, and Elinor and Marianne Dashwood in the 1811 book *Sense and Sensibility*, where the differences between the characters, who are established as opposites in the book's title, are central to the novel and form the key narrative device through which Austen establishes the character arcs of the two protagonists. Another pervasive example can be seen in the long-running cartoon series *The Simpsons* (created by Matt Groening for the Fox Broadcasting Company in 1989), in which sibling characters Bart and Lisa Simpson are depicted as opposites, with Bart the mischievous, fun-loving boy who, like his father, lacks academic intelligence, constructed in contrast to his clever, sensible and mature sister Lisa. In her 1996 novel *Never Far from Nowhere*, Andrea Levy tells the story of black Caribbean sisters whose experiences of growing up in London in the 1970s are shaped by appearance, with Vivien having much lighter skin than her sister Olive. Levy's novel, told from both sisters' perspectives, explores how their relationships, education and feelings of belonging are moulded by their different experiences of racism and colourism.

Tropes about people, particularly women, with no siblings are also commonly used in fiction to create absorbing characters and to explain their unique traits. Rosemary M. Colt identifies how lone female children in novels are often portrayed as taking 'control of their destinies' 'against great odds' (1993: 11). Colt describes only children in literature as '[v]ulnerable but resilient, they are lone innocents in a world scornful of or threatened by their presence' (1993: 11). Drawing on Charlotte Brontë's portrayal of the single female child in her 1847 novel *Jane Eyre*, Colt demonstrates how these figures 'discomfit the adult world' (1993: 11), offering a commentary on adults' lives from a place of disconcerting innocence in a way more pronounced than in portrayals of children with siblings.

These fictional siblings and 'only children' demonstrate something of the intrigue and mystery of siblingship, as relationships imbued with emotional extremes and where similarities and differences between siblings are fascinating narrative devices to manipulate. Some of this intrigue is present in media preoccupations with celebrity siblings. The idea that sibling relationships are often imbued with jealousy certainly captures the public imagination, and we see this in the media fascination with rivalries between political brothers such as the US Kennedy dynasty, who were described in the *Irish Times* as being 'pushed' and 'groomed' for political success by their parents (Haas, 2021). Brothers George W. and Jeb Bush were similarly described in the *Los Angeles Times* as having 'a complex relationship, marked by fierce rivalry, wounded feelings' (Barabak, 2015). In British politics, sibling rivalries have also courted media attention; brothers Ed and David Miliband's 2010 competition for the position of leader of the Labour Party inspired headlines such as 'A Tale of Brotherly Love: When Siblings Fall Out, and Try to Make Up' (Bennett, 2010) and the listing of infamous fraternal rivals in the headline, 'Romulus and Remus, Prospero and Antonio, David and Ed…' (Higgins, 2010). Similarly, the story of Prime Minister Boris Johnson's brother, Jo, who resigned his ministerial role in 2019 after a row about Brexit, sparked speculation about the emotional consequences of a dispute between brothers, with the *Evening Standard* running the headline, 'Blow for Bojo as Bro Jo Go Goes' and the *Daily Mirror* going with 'Even Boris' Own Family Don't Trust Him'.

Other famous sibling relationships have also fascinated the public such as that between British princes William and Harry, where speculation about their once presumed 'closeness' and subsequent 'rift' has inspired countless newspaper articles, blogs, books, film and television documentaries. Toureille's article in the *Mail Online* in September 2021 is typical in its dissection of every public exchange between the brothers: 'Prince William's "Curt" Message to Prince Harry on his Birthday Showed their Relationship is still "Icy" and They Are no Closer to Making Up, Royal Experts Claim'; the *Evening Standard* ran the following headline in July 2021: 'Brothers at War: Can William and Harry Heal their Rift?' There have been books and television documentary series based on the so-called feud between the princes, such as Robert Lacey's 2020 book *Battle of Brothers: William, Harry and the Inside Story of a Family in Tumult* and the 2021 Passionate Eye documentary, 'Harry and William: What Went Wrong?'

One of the key reasons why sibling relationships are so intriguing is that they seem to hold some of the mysteries of what it means to be human, helping us to ponder the conundrum of the relative influences of 'nature' – such as 'blood' ties or genetic inheritance – and 'nurture' – how we are raised, a sense of the environment in which we live. In turn this gives rise to questions about what is fixed and what is malleable about how we 'turn out' in life. How far are our character, personality, ways of being, health, intelligence or success determined by our genes or by our upbringing? Siblings seem to encapsulate some of these mysteries, and we employ our own expertise in kinship and how things are 'passed on' (Edwards, 2000; Mason, 2008) to figure out what it means when siblings look alike (does it follow that they will be alike in other ways too?) and how siblings who share talents or aptitudes came to possess their 'gifts'. We might ask why siblings who share genetic heritage and who are raised in the same home by the same parents might turn out to be different. This fascination extends to an appetite for seeking formulas to explain how different configurations of sibship might affect the ways we turn out in life. Are youngest siblings more likely to be 'free thinkers'? Are eldest children more likely to become leaders? Does being an only child make someone better at working alone?

I am asked such questions every time I give a media interview on siblingship, and of course the intricacies of family life, diverse forms of sibling relationships and complexities of socio-economic influence mean that they cannot be answered sociologically (in the following chapter I consider the sorts of academic questions that are and can be asked about siblingship). However, it should not be surprising that these questions are fascinating. Sibling relationships can be so important (even 'only children' grow up with the sense of *not* having siblings) that we are bound to wonder how they affect us. The practice of comparing siblings and the interest gained from focusing on differences between siblings (for example in the Jane Austen novels and *The Simpsons* cartoon discussed above) mean we often live with a sense of ourselves *in relation* to our siblings (see K. Davies, 2015). These quite profound questions about how siblings 'turn out' can also be seen in interest in celebrity siblings. Think of the US tennis stars sisters Venus and Serena Williams, who have each won numerous Grand Slam tournaments and have both occupied the position of the Women's Tennis Association's number

1 player. We might wonder where their incredible talent came from. How much was down to the luck of genetics and how much was a result of them having access to opportunities to play tennis at an early age or being coached by their father? These questions might be intertwined with curiosity about their emotional relationship – how did it feel to compete against one another, playing one another in the finals of huge competitions such as Wimbledon?

Many of these questions about nature versus nurture, resemblance and connection are even more closely linked to the intrigue of twinship. Though twins are not the focus of this book, the public fascination with twins, the continuing prevalence of twin studies as a method in psychological studies and the representation of twins in popular culture means they help to illuminate some of the aspects that make siblings intriguing. Elizabeth Stewart (2000) points to the prevalence of myths about twinship, from biblical depictions of twins including Esau and Jacob, whose struggle begins in the womb and whose relationship is defined by differences between them, to twins such as Romulus and Remus, founders of Rome, whose rivalry resulted in Romulus killing his twin brother. Such myths around twinship are centred on key ideas about difference, resemblance, struggle and rivalry.

The characteristics of siblingship that have captured the public imagination also partly explain why siblings are interesting to think about and with sociologically. Ideas about what siblingship means become entwined with how people make sense of their own experience of being or having siblings – or not having siblings. However, sociological tools can also help us to interrogate these, moving beyond simplistic representations of siblings to consider the diversity of sibling ties and the complexities involved in defining siblingship.

What is a sibling?

Despite the plethora of media depictions of sibling relationships and the prevalence of stereotypes about what siblingship ought to look like, defining siblings is not straightforward. Of course, the diversity of family forms (according to the Office for National Statistics, in 2011 nearly one in ten children in England and Wales were living with a step-family) means that the term 'sibling' needs to include full siblings (who share the same genetic parents), step-siblings (who are related through the marriage of one of their parents but are not genetically related) and half-siblings (who share one genetic parent), as well as siblings related through adoption, fostering, donor gametes and relationships that can feel like sibling relationships even when the individuals are not related by blood or marriage. These sibling-like relationships often include features such as generational proximity, a sense of a shared childhood, of companionship or support, even bickering and arguing, which are often seen to pertain to siblings in some way. However, even these features of siblingship are not straightforward. Large age gaps or the acquisition of step- or half-siblings through parents' re-partnering can mean that siblings do not always occupy similar generational locations in the historical sense (Mannheim, 1952), and, as described in relation to my own experiences of lockdown, wider socio-economic shifts and policy decisions as well as changes in the circumstances of individual families can mean that, even if siblings are relatively close in age, they do not necessarily grow up 'together' in the historical generational sense. This also relates to the assumption that siblings share the same 'environment' in terms of the 'nature versus nurture' conundrum. Even if siblings do share the same genetic parentage and grow up together in the same household at the same time, the family environment will be experienced differently by each member, who will each have their own configuration of relationships viewed and experienced from their own unique vantage point.

Similarly, despite the interest in birth order and how it might affect the ways people turn out in terms of their personality, education, occupation, skills and talents, birth order is not static. Children in reconstituted families may find themselves occupying different birth-order positions in each parent's home depending on the presence of step- or half-siblings. People who grow up with a large age gap between themselves and their younger sibling(s) might have been an only child for a significant period of their childhood, while those who have much older siblings may feel that they have grown up effectively as only children, with their older siblings no longer living in the family home for much of their childhood. Samantha Punch (2008) has also demonstrated, in her study of sibships of three children in Scotland, that birth-order roles are negotiated and contested within full sibling relationships. Furthermore, gendered differences in sibling relationships are not necessarily fixed. Though the data on which much of this book draws do not contain trans, non-binary or gender fluid-identifying siblings, we know that, though it is common to refer to 'brothers' and 'sisters' in popular parlance, these categories are not mutually exclusive.

It might seem, given these diversities and complexities, that defining siblings is a fruitless task. However, following David Morgan's (1996; 2011) concept of 'family practices' – which identifies 'family' as a verb, rather than a noun – it is possible to see siblingship as something that is *done,* and a family relationship as something that is created through the repetition of everyday family activities. As such, 'family actors are not simply persons defined as mothers, fathers and so on but they can also be seen as "doing" mothering or fathering' (Morgan, 2011: 6). Thus siblings can be created through *doing* siblingship. According to Morgan, family practices are 'often little fragments of daily life which are part of the normal taken-for-granted existence of the practitioners. Their significance derives from their location in wider systems of meaning' (1996: 189–90). So, we can define sibling practices as created in relationships as well as through wider societal agreements about what constitutes siblingship. Morgan argues that these practices,

> appear to have a natural or given character, something which is recognised in many folk expressions about family relations and obligations. Part of the complex process of the construction of family practices is that such practices often seem natural, inevitable and significant to the parties involved. (1996: 192)

This means that sibling relationships might seem to be dictated by blood or marriage, and the practices they involve (arguing, for example, or caring, or sharing a childhood home) might seem to be a taken-for-granted product of this tie. However, for sibling practices, the tangling of lived experience with normative assumptions may be more open to negotiation than with other family practices, such as mothering or fathering. Sibling relationships are less scripted than intergenerational relationships between parents and children and, though they have a clear presence in the popular imagination, tropes and stereotypes about sibling relationships are a bundle of contradictions comprising emotions such as love and jealousy, practices such as care and fighting, and with individual siblings defined by labels of both similarity and difference. Sibling practices also differ according to age, class, gender and ethnicity and are shaped by parents' own experiences and expectations of sibling relationships. Sibling relationships may also be lived at a distance or across borders. This means that sibling relationships, as well as being practised, are also imagined and remembered.

Thinking *about* siblings

In thinking about siblings as the entwining of everyday practices and normative tropes as well as being shaped by memories and emotions, it is helpful to draw upon concepts of relationality, which emphasise how personal relationships can shape people's lives and identities. Thinking about siblingship in terms of relationality helps us to see how seemingly individual 'practices and identities [are] embedded within webs of relationships' (Mason, 2004: 177). Jennifer Mason highlights the presence of 'relational thinking' (2004: 177) in the ways personal decisions are made, and Carol Smart emphasises how relationships can form 'a context for the unfolding of everyday life' (2007: 49). In her discussion of this relational understanding of personal life, Smart brings together emotions, memory, biography and imagination to demonstrate how we are embedded in webs of relationships that span time and space. For Smart, this approach focuses on 'what matters to people in the construction of their everyday lives' and acknowledges agency without 'extract[ing] the person from their embeddedness in history, tradition, biography and relationships' (2007: 187). This means that we can envision sibling relationships as interwoven with other relationships and contexts (for example, in my personal reflections on siblingship in lockdown where sibling relationships in childhood and adulthood were entwined with relationships to parents, normative ideas about the 'goods' of being and having siblings, and the wider sociocultural context). Particularly pertinent for sibling relationships – which can involve arguing, fighting, irritation and jealousy as well as more positive characteristics – Smart also points to the importance of relationships that are not always experienced as positive ties, highlighting how even negative or estranged relationships can be 'sticky' because 'it is hard to shake free from them at an emotional level and their existence can continue to influence our practices and not just our thoughts' (2007: 45).

In her discussions of relationality and kinship, Mason (2008; 2018) emphasises the physical, sensory, material and ethereal elements of these sticky connections between relatives. She highlights the importance of aspects of relatedness that can sometimes seem to be outside the sociological remit, arguing that 'real life kinship involves ethereal and sensory dimensions, whether or not sociologists are used to exploring these' (2008: 43). However peripheral to sociological inquiry they might seem, these elements are central to understandings of what it means to be related, and often induce public fascination. Mason emphasises how affinities between kin contain 'different dimensions of fixity, creativity, ethereality and materiality and the sensory' (2008: 42), and we have seen how these tangible and intangible affinities and the conundrum of the role of genetics in creating relationships are present in siblingship, from the embodied nature of my children's sibling relationship described in the opening to this book to the mysteries of nature and nurture and of resemblances seen in the public fascination with siblingship.

Sasha Roseneil and Kaisa Ketokivi also take ideas of relationality in a direction particularly pertinent to understanding sibling relationships, by pointing to how people reflect upon themselves as individuals in relation to others; what they term the 'agentic reflexivity of the relational person' (2006: 148). As an individual who is also one in a series, a sibling – perhaps more than other relational forms – 'gains its identity and becomes "what" it is in relation to surrounding persons, places, meanings and events' (Roseneil and Ketokivi, 2006: 148).

Thus, relationality, or, as Smart terms it, the 'connectedness thesis' (2007: 189), is a useful toolkit of ideas to help to think through siblingship sociologically. These are unpacked in detail in Chapter 3, but the conceptualisation of people as relational beings who make sense of who they are and what they do as part of a web of relationships with others spanning time and space permeates all the analyses that follow, and is central to my theorisation of sibling relationships and why they matter.

Another idea that is fundamental to the arguments presented in this book is the central tenet of the revolution in sociological understandings of childhood pioneered by Alan Prout and Allison James (1997); that of the agentic child who is conceptualised as 'being' in the present rather than analytically reduced to who they might 'become'. Though siblings are often thought of as synonymous with childhood, one of the key contributions of this book is that it moves beyond a focus on children's sibling relationships, taking a life course perspective which explores how siblingship ebbs and flows over time. However, the simple idea of the agentic child helps to push thinking about siblingship into new territory by un-privileging the parent–child relationship in the analysis. By focusing on the agency of children (both in childhood as well as in adolescence and adulthood), it is possible to explore the significance of lateral ties in the ways we turn out. For example, we can privilege the role of siblings in our understandings of the transference of capital, in the experience of the life course, in the shaping of the social self and in the provision of care.

The chapters that follow use these framings to situate a sociology of siblings, illustrating why and how siblings matter in people's lives and therefore why they are deserving of further sociological scrutiny. In so doing the book moves beyond these frameworks to explore the role of siblingship in other key areas of sociological thought, drawing together literatures familiar to sociology such as those on self and identity, emotion, care, normativity and morality, age, time and the life course as well as ideas about sensorial, embodied and otherworldly connections. In using these literatures to think about siblings and why they are so important, the book in turn uses siblings as a lens through which to look differently at key sociological ideas, offering a new perspective on familiar themes that have been central to the discipline: self, relationality, imagination and time.

Thinking *with* siblings

The chapters of this book will demonstrate why siblings matter sociologically, unpacking some of the key features of siblingship to explore their significance. Taking these discussions as a point of departure, the book then goes further, examining how these features of siblingship make siblings a useful sociological tool to think with, illuminating novel ways of approaching key themes such as self, relationality, normativity and temporality, offering different perspectives on some of these central tenets of sociological thought.

As such, the main arguments in this book are structured around four key sociological themes: self, relationality, imagination and time. In each chapter, I discuss the sociological significance of siblingship in relation to these themes, unpacking how we can think about the significance of sibling relationships as well as how some of the particularities of siblingship can help us develop sociological thinking in these areas.

The aspects of siblingship that make them important and intriguing also make them fruitful to think with. Sociological thinking about the self has tended to focus on processes of socialisation, and as such, identification with adults, particularly parents, has been central. Looking at siblings helps us to recognise the importance of lateral ties in shaping the self, directing the gaze not only horizontally as well as vertically in the search for sources of social influence, but also conceiving of webs of relationships of influence. This shift in ways of looking and thinking about the relational constitution of the self illuminates *how* these relational processes occur within the complexities of relationship dynamics, attending to power and personal politics as they are lived within the nexus of those inter- and intragenerational relationships in which people are embedded.

Kinship is often described by anthropologists as the place where nature and nurture combine, and Marilyn Strathern conceptualises English kinship in terms of 'merographic connections' (1992: 72), with kinship comprised of parts of different wholes. For example, kin names such as 'sibling' belong to the domain (or whole) of the social but are also part of biology – the names of gametes after all belong to the realms of science. These parts, which belong to different wholes, mingle in kinship, which in turn is understood as inherently containing a mix of the natural and the social (see also Franklin, 2003). Sociological approaches to relationality have traditionally paid less attention to the realm of biology or nature, though there are some important studies which do consider these matters (Mason, 2008; Nordqvist, 2017). Studying siblings, intriguing precisely because they cut right to the heart of these issues, can help us to consider the significance of 'nature' versus 'nurture' debates sociologically. Siblings are, after all, where key questions about the mechanisms of nature and culture in how we turn out are often made most visible or observable. Thinking with siblings also brings other issues into our understandings of relationality and encourages us to think about how care can be provided in relationships that may be complex and contradictory (featuring, for example, love, hate, aggression or jealousy) and how relationships can be experienced and performed differently in different contexts (such as in the home, at school, in the local neighbourhood or at after-school clubs). The physicality and embodied nature of many sibling relationships can also help to push sociological analyses of relationships along less well-trodden paths.

The role of imagination in sociological thought is often understood in terms of normativity, and in studies of familial relationships this often translates to the concept of idealised relational forms or behaviours that it is imagined one must somehow live up to. Thinking with siblings helps to illuminate gaps between normative expectations and everyday realities of relationships. Sibling relationships are relatively unscripted in comparison to relationship roles such as those occupied by parents, but are still influenced by normative ideas about what a sibling ought to do or be, as well as those ideas about how siblings ought to be treated that were discussed in my account of parenting siblings in lockdown. These imagined ideal siblings are often contradicted by the ambivalence of many people's sibling relationships, and these gaps help illuminate and unpack the messy and nuanced ways that normative ideas are negotiated in everyday life.

Thinking with siblings also encourages the amalgamation of different facets of temporality usually discussed separately in socio-logical accounts of time. Understanding meanings and experiences of siblingship necessitates the combining of ideas about calendar time, life course transitions and generation. For example, siblings often have lateral relationships – and are assumed to be of the same generation – yet, as we saw in my reflections on the different experi-ences and legal rights of my two children during the COVID-19 UK lockdowns, even siblings close in calendar age may find themselves navigating quite different socio-economic environments or politi-cal and policy landscapes, as well as shifts or ruptures at a more micro level. Furthermore, the importance of calendar age can wax and wane, as sibling relationships can feel more or less 'lateral' at

different points in the life course, or in different contexts such as
at school or home where the meaning of birth order and age gap
can shift. These complexities help to bring the relational nature of
life course transitions into focus, illuminating the complexities of
sociological categories such as age and generation and demonstrating
how they interact with individual biographies and socio-economic
and political eras.

Following a discussion of the sorts of academic questions that
have been asked about siblings, this book is structured around these
four concepts of self, rationality, imagination and time. These themes
have been selected because of their centrality to the discipline as
well as their pertinence to sibling relationships in particular, helping
to further understandings of why sibling relationships matter. In
pointing to these four themes, the book makes an important contribution to sociology – progressing and extending a sociology of siblings
while also contributing to ideas that are more familiar topics of
sociological concern. Of course, there are other themes that are
important and that might also have been considered as constituting
separate chapters. Gender, geography and ethnicity, for example,
are all important themes that are threaded through the chapters of
this book and that, though the data were not available to explore
them in more depth here, all warrant further study.

About this book

The data

In laying out the significance of siblings and demonstrating the value
in asking sociological questions with and about siblings, this book
draws on two datasets, along with a wide range of other academic
literatures. The first is a series of focus groups and qualitative
interviews with young people conducted by me in the UK between
2007 and 2008. The second is a collection of written responses to
a Mass Observation Project directive which asked the established
panel of the UK archive's lay writers (mass observers) to respond
to a series of prompts about sibling relationships. I commissioned
the Mass Observation Project directive with funds provided by the
Morgan Centre for the Study of Everyday Life at the University of

Manchester in 2012. These studies were conducted a number of years before the writing of this book and the data were reanalysed for the purposes of this volume. Of course, the cultural contexts in which these data were generated were quite different from those experienced by siblings today. Furthermore, the data are confined to the UK context. However, this book is not intended to be a research monograph reporting on the findings from these studies; rather these data are put to work to craft a sociology of siblingship, and ideas from these accounts are put into conversation with a wide range of other sociological literatures to think about the meanings of siblingship in ways not confined to the temporal and cultural contexts in which the accounts were generated.

The dataset of focus groups conducted in schools with young people comprised nine groups with 75 young people (33 girls, 42 boys, aged between 11 and 14 years old), and 26 qualitative interviews with 41 young people (17 boys and 24 girls) within the same age range, conducted in schools, homes and youth clubs. Some interviews were with individuals, some (particularly those conducted in youth clubs) were with groups of two or three friends. Young people were able to decide whether they wanted to be interviewed alone or with friends. Parents were sometimes present during interviews in homes and occasionally took part in the discussion. Young people had less choice about whether their parent was present. The dynamics of these exchanges are discussed at points throughout this book. Participants were recruited from three schools in the north of England, selected to access young people from a mix of ethnic and economic backgrounds: 'Highfields' and 'Romsbridge' (both large comprehensive schools with economically mixed catchment areas) and 'St Stephen's' (a small Roman Catholic secondary school in a deprived area). Four focus groups were carried out at Highfields school and five at St Stephen's. All the young people who took part in focus groups were invited to participate in a follow-up interview. The interview sample was then boosted through recruitment drives at Romsbridge school and at three youth clubs: the 'Freedom Centre' (a specialist arts centre), an estate youth club (situated on a deprived housing estate) and a rural youth club (in an affluent rural village). During my time at the Freedom Centre, I volunteered for one week during a children's holiday club that took place during the school summer holidays, and in this time I conducted participant observation with the young people who attended. My field notes from this period of observation form part of this dataset and are discussed in Chapter 3.

Though participants were often unable to provide sufficient details of their parents' occupations to facilitate classification by standard occupation-based social class categories, the different fieldwork sites provide indications of the social locations of participants. Classed narratives of privilege, ambition and deprivation were particularly important in the context of the housing estate, where young people commonly spoke about their perceived lack of job and educational opportunities, and in the rural youth club and mixed catchment schools where participants often alluded to the desirability of apparently middle-class trajectories involving university and a 'professional' career. There were 27 non-white focus group participants and 9 non-white interviewees who defined their ethnicity in a short questionnaire as 'mixed race', 'black British' or 'Asian British'. The arts-based youth club was particularly diverse and emphasised Caribbean-influenced art, music and dance. Despite the small numbers of young people in each ethnic group, there were interesting narratives about the role of ethnic, cultural and religious norms surrounding sibling relationships. The sample contained very few young people who did not have siblings (just one interview participant and four focus group participants), and many young people in the sample had complex combinations of full, step- and half-siblings of various ages and living in different households. None of the young people in the study expressly identified as transsexual or non-binary, but these terms were less widely used or understood at the time of the study, and I did not ask young people directly about this, though they were able to write their self-defined gender in an open questionnaire.

The aims of this project as a whole were to explore how young people's relationships impacted upon their understandings of how they were 'turning out', not just at school but in terms of their sense of personhood more generally. An exploration of the role of sibling relationships in these processes was built into the design of the project from the beginning, and the analysis presented in this book is derived from the aspects of the interviews and focus groups that covered sibling relationships. In interviews, young people who had siblings were asked about their experiences of these relationships, as well as how they felt they were similar to or different from their siblings. Many young people also discussed their cousins or the siblings of their friends. Focus group discussions included more normative questions about the advantages and disadvantages of being or having siblings – including a discussion of gender and birth-order roles, whether and how siblings can turn out to be similar or different from one another and how siblings ought to be treated by others, particularly parents and teachers. Participants were also shown a clip from the *Simpsons* cartoon series from an episode titled 'Bart Gets an F'. The clip dealt with Bart's response to his sister getting yet another 'A' on a school report while he was struggling academically. The clip was used as a vignette in focus groups to spark discussion about the emotional implications of similarities and differences between siblings and the moralities of how they ought to be parented.

Data were analysed using thematic and narrative analytical techniques and coded according to key themes, many of which emerged during analysis, such as resemblance, sibling roles and emotional aspects of similarities and differences between siblings. This thematic analysis was combined with in-depth analyses of individual cases to better understand the context and narrative formation of young people's stories. It was not always possible to ascertain who was speaking in focus group discussions, as can be seen from the extracts that are cited throughout the chapters that follow.[1]

The second dataset is a collection of 171 written responses to a Mass Observation Project directive on siblings commissioned by me in the summer of 2012. Mass observers are a pool of UK-based lay writers who regularly respond to directives from Mass Observation on a wide range of themes, from their experiences of political or national events such as Brexit or the Queen's Jubilee, to 'day in the life' accounts and topics commissioned by academics such as 'Belonging' or 'Difficult Friendships'. The respondents to my directive were aged between 17 and 92, though the panel is well known to be skewed towards older people. This proved useful for my purposes as it enabled me to move beyond a consideration of siblingship in childhood and to take a more life course perspective, incorporating the views and experiences of older people. Though details of respondents' gender and age are available, and often some sort of information about their occupation and/or social class background is provided, it was not always possible to ascertain other important details such as ethnicity. Several volunteer writers for the Mass Observation Project have written for the archive for many years and are well versed and often skilled in constructing a narrative and writing for posterity (Davies and Heaphy, 2011; Sheridan, 1993). Writers were provided with a set of prompts but were free to write as much or as little as they wanted and could respond to and interpret the prompts freely. The prompts provided for the siblings directive were as follows:

The focus of the second part of the Directive is sibling relationships (including full, half, step and adopted siblings and those who are 'like' siblings). We are interested in your views and experiences of having brothers or sisters, particularly in terms of how these relationships adapt and change as you grow older.

The first section of this Directive is aimed at people who have siblings. If you don't have a sibling we would welcome your thoughts and observations about friends, family members or acquaintances that do have siblings.

If you have a sibling: Please start by listing your siblings. How are they related to you? We would like to hear about full, half, step and adopted siblings and others who may be 'like' siblings in some way. Please describe your siblings (without identifying them by name) – how old are they? What do they do? What are they like?

Your relationship with your siblings: How would you describe your relationship with your siblings? How often do you see/speak to your siblings? Has this changed over time? Have there been times when you have been very close or experienced rivalry or resentment with your siblings? Please give as much detail as possible.

Do you and your siblings ever help each other out? This could be in the form of emotional support, advice, financial help or something similar. Can you imagine a time in the future when you might give or receive this type of help? Have you ever lost contact with a sibling? What happened? Similarities and differences: Are you similar or different to your siblings? This could be in terms of appearance, personality, health, character and so on. Have you got any theories about how these similarities/differences came about? Have these similarities/differences changed over time?

If you have more than one sibling... Are you closer to one particular sibling? Why is this? Has this changed at all over the years? Have there been times when age differences or birth order have seemed important to you and your siblings.

Finding siblings in later life: Do you have any experience of finding out about siblings in later life? Please share any experience that is relevant to you or other people that you know.

For everybody: What do you think the advantages and disadvantages of growing up without siblings are? Have you ever wished you had/did not have any brothers or sisters? Do you think your life would be any different if you had/did not have any siblings? Do you have any thoughts and opinions on how siblings 'turn out'? For example, do you think that eldest children, people from large families or people with no siblings tend to 'turn out' differently? What makes you think this?

The responses varied greatly, with a mixture of handwritten and word-processed responses which included long stories and reflections of childhood memories, potted life stories, bullet point responses to each section of the directive and curt responses of just a sentence or two. In order to analyse the dataset, I read though each response and noted key themes. I then selected a sub-sample of 30 responses – including a mix of different 'styles' of reply but otherwise choosing at random – to analyse in more depth and use as a basis for a case study-driven analysis. The findings from these analyses inform the use of the Mass Observation Project data in this book, which is interspersed with accounts from the young people who took part in interviews and focus groups. Mass observers' accounts are drawn upon particularly in Chapter 5, which deals with time, as many respondents were able to reflect on their experiences of siblingship from childhood through to adulthood and, in many cases, into old age.

Thus, rather than forming a monograph explicitly about either of these research projects, the book weaves together case studies and cross-sectional analyses from focus groups, interviews, observational notes and mass observers' written reflections, along with examples from popular culture, literature and academic texts from sociology and beyond, in order to put siblings on the sociological map and illustrate why they matter sociologically.

The structure of the book

Set against an acknowledgement of the lack of attention paid to siblings in sociology, Chapter 1 explores some of the empirical and theoretical questions that have been asked about siblings in different disciplines. The chapter covers siblings in psychology, where questions about the influence of siblings on childhood development and the continued use of twin study methodologies mean that siblings have been more central to the discipline than we have seen in sociology. The chapter goes on to explore the use of siblings as a variable in various quantitative studies which seek to identify formulas about how aspects of siblingship – such as birth order, number of siblings or age gap – affect the ways people 'turn out' in life in terms of outcomes, such as educational attainment. A more sociological focus on the quality of sibling relationships themselves is identified in work that asks questions about caring for vulnerable siblings, particularly in terms of fostering or adoption, as well as the effects of having a disabled sibling on relationships and responsibilities. Moving to look directly at sociological approaches, the chapter then outlines the small but important body of work that has applied sociological questions about sibling relationships; questions about the role of siblings in shaping identity and the social construction of sibling roles and relationships. The chapter concludes by considering questions about how sibling relationships may be experienced differently according to cultural and ethnic diversity and in different global contexts.

Chapter 2 covers the relationship between siblingship and sociological understandings of the self. The chapter begins with an extended discussion of the narratives of two sisters, Anna and Francesca. Their stories emphasise how personalities, talents and attributes, as well as experiences of school, friendships and so on, are constructed in opposition to one another so that the differences between them are emphasised and used to inform a sense of a fixed, essential self. The chapter then draws upon wider interview and focus group data, along with mass observers' accounts, to discuss the relational construction of sibling identity, demonstrating how siblings are constructed in relation to how they are similar to or different from one another. Siblings also influence each other's experience of key life events and institutions, such as education, where older siblings often provide a 'foil' by which younger siblings measure and evaluate their own experience. The chapter outlines how people both construct themselves and are constructed by others in relation to their similarities to or differences from their siblings, and draws upon theories of the discursive construct of the culture of the 'authentic', 'inner' self to address the paradox between being an individual and being one in a series of siblings. The chapter goes on to explore the role of stories in generating narratives of similarity and difference, unpacking the interpersonal politics and power dynamics of the telling and retelling of family stories. The chapter concludes with an exploration of how the relational construction of sibling identity can work through the 'carrying over' or 'rubbing off' of siblings' reputations in various contexts such as school and home, highlighting how this is enhanced by the public perception of physical resemblances between siblings.

Chapter 3 explores the meanings and experiences of relationships between siblings. The chapter begins with a consideration of the complexities and contradictions of sibling relationships, which are often characterised by a unique combination of care and annoyance. Drawing on Julie Brownlie's (2014) concept of 'being there', the chapter uses data from interviews and focus groups with young people along with mass observers' narratives to explore the kinds of background being there that characterise many sibling relationships. The chapter goes on to consider the creation of siblingship through sibling practices, exploring how siblings come to feel 'real' or not, emphasising the work that can go into creating a 'sibling-like' relationship. The chapter examines the embodied and sensory close-ness that characterises many sibling relationships, particularly in childhood. These include physical fighting, which is entangled with the day-to-day irritations of siblingship, as well as other forms of sensorial closeness such as memories of particular smells or of the sensation of a hug. The book draws on different sources, including participant observation at a holiday club, to explore how siblingship is practised in the contexts of home, school, holiday clubs and the local community. The chapter ends with a discussion of more ethereal elements – uncanny resemblances or strange connections and coincidences rooted in a deep sort of knowing.

Chapter 4 moves on from these experiential aspects of siblingship to consider imaginings of idealised or yearned-for sibling relationships. The chapter begins by exploring siblings' sense of their roles and responsibilities, which are closely linked to gender and birth order, drawing upon John Gillis's (1997) differential between the idealised families we live by and the realities of the families we live with, to examine gaps between normative ideals and lived realities of sibling relationships. The chapter draws on the account of two friends as they discuss their different experiences of and feelings about wanting more siblings on the one hand, and the messy realities of being from a big family on the other. The case study demonstrates how normativity, morality, lived relationalities and imagination interweave in siblingship. The chapter then goes on to explore yearned-for or imagined siblings, using Susie Scott's work on the sociology of nothing (2018; 2019) to understand the nature of sibling relationships through a consideration of what it means not to have a sibling. The chapter concludes with a discussion of lay expertise in kinship, considering how assumptions about how kinship works implicate everyday theorising about how one might 'turn out' as a sibling.

Chapter 5 explores the temporal facets of siblingship, from the ways the experience and importance of sibling relationships may shift through the life course to the fluidity of birth order and age gap. The chapter begins with an in-depth discussion of one mass observer's account of her sibling relationships, exploring the ways in which the observer narrates these experiences through a temporal lens – tracking memories, change over time, pivotal moments as well as imagining what the future might bring. The chapter then considers a wider range of data to explore how siblings can form a 'temporal convoy' (Gillis, 1997) – a long-term presence as we make our way through life – and draws on the accounts of mass observers who pointed to the importance of sibling support that could be reactivated at particular moments (such as in the event of a parent's death) following a fallow period. The chapter explores people's narratives of how they have 'turned out' in life in relation to their siblings, which continue even after the intense period of comparing that characterises many children's sibling relationships has diminished. This is linked to the idea that many siblings share a sort of 'privileged knowledge' (Jamieson, 1998) formed through shared childhood experiences, rendering them uniquely able to understand the difficulties of caring for ageing parents. The chapter engages with ideas about generation, exploring what it means for siblings to be generationally proximate, as well as pointing to how siblings who are close in age may experience different socio-economic eras which impact on their lives in various ways. The chapter concludes by using siblings to consider the socially constructed and relational nature of age by revealing how birth order and age gap may shift in meaning over time.

The book concludes with an overview of the benefits for sociology of thinking both about and with siblings. The conclusion explores the role of siblings in processes of turning out, and suggests area of future research, particularly concerning power and diversity in the experiences and meanings of siblingship.

Note

1 Pseudonyms have been adopted for all the young people and institutions featured in this book.

Chapter 1

Asking questions about siblingship

How are sibling relationships experienced, imagined and understood through the life course? How does being and having siblings affect our sense of self and our experience of social institutions such as school, work and family? How are sibling relationships imagined and how are understandings of age, birth order and gender in sibships constructed in different contexts?

These are just some of the sociological questions we might want to ask about siblings, and there exists a small but significant body of work within the sociology of family which empirically addresses some of these questions. However, questions of siblingship remain on the periphery of the discipline, and work on key sociological themes such as socialisation, life course 'transitions', the construction of self/identity and the transmission of social advantage has tended to focus on parents as the primary source of social influence, neglecting the role of siblings in these processes. This preoccupation with intergenerational transmission perhaps reflects the historically important role of sociology in highlighting the social reproduction of (dis)advantage and of analytically rooting inequality in social structures, whereby an analysis of capital as passing *down* the generations has been an important tool in countering a focus on individual blame.

Many of the empirical questions posed by scholars about siblingship come from disciplines outside sociology and relate to the impact of siblings on child development (Sanders, 2004), or consider siblings as a variable in quantitative studies which seek to measure siblings' effect on various outcomes such as educational qualifications. Consequently, academic studies of siblingship have tended to be dominated by psychological questions pertaining to the effect of being and, mainly, having a sibling or siblings on individual development (Edwards et al., 2006). Siblings have also featured in anthropological studies of more broadly defined kin networks in various, often non-Western cultural contexts, though often as a consequence of broader questions around kinship structures rather than as an object of interest in their own right.

Scholars working in other disciplines beyond psychology have pointed to a similar neglect of siblings. Juliet Mitchell, for example, decries the neglect of siblings in psychoanalytic thought, which she equates with a focus on the child in the context of their relationships with adults. As we have seen in sociology, this has resulted in the foregrounding of vertical relationships with parents in much psychoanalytic theorising. Mitchell writes:

> The proposition here is this: that an observation of the importance of siblings, and all the lateral relations that take their cue from them, must lead to a paradigm shift that challenges the unique importance of understanding through vertical paradigms. Mothers and fathers are, of course, immensely important, but social life does not only follow from a relationship with them as it is made to do in our Western theories. (2003: 3)

Mitchell goes on to explore the centrality of siblings to key tenets of psychoanalytical theory, such as the development of the ego-ideal and conceptualisations of hysteria. Through her feminist analysis, Mitchell suggests that the dominance of vertical relationships in psychoanalysis 'has arisen because human social and individual psychology has been understood from the side of the man' (2003: 3) with a focus on the Oedipal father rather than the peer (2003: 13). For Mitchell, opening up psychoanalytical thinking to look at the importance of lateral ties steps away from the focus on men and creates opportunities for different ways of conceptualising the development of the psyche.

Prophecy Coles also points to the oversimplification of the Oedipus complex as a 'fulcrum of our psychic development' (2003: 2) in psychoanalytic thought, and similarly emphasises the importance of horizontal ties with siblings and peers, which, she argues, do important but often overlooked work in shaping the psyche, helping us to break free from the dominance of our parents, showing us how to relate in different ways. For Coles, like Mitchell, parents are 'only half the story of our emotional development' (2003: 2): 'The feelings we have towards our siblings have an important place in the complexity of our life, and to dismiss their significance is to impoverish our internal world' (Coles, 2003: 2). Some of these psychoanalytically inspired questions about the role of horizontal ties with siblings on our inner emotional lives have been applied to sociological research, and I return to these later in this chapter.

Social historian Leonore Davidoff similarly notes that siblings have been a taken-for-granted, 'absent presence' (2012: 1) in historical studies of families and familial relationships, which have tended to focus on the simplistic question, 'Was it better or worse for people in the past?' (2012: 4). Davidoff observes that siblings are finally starting to attract some attention among historians at a time in the West when, due to changes in fertility rates, people have fewer siblings than ever before. Like many sociologists who have discussed the importance of siblingship, Davidoff points to the long-lasting nature of sibling ties when considering their significance:

> For while parents die, friends drift in and out, marriages and partner-ships dissolve, children – if there are any – leave, for those that have them, brothers and sisters remain an inextricable part of existence from our earliest world. In adult life they may never be in contact but they cannot be formally divorced. In a sense, brothers and sisters are *life's longest relationship*. (2012: 2, original emphasis)

Davidoff goes on to explore the role of siblings in British middle-class families in the 'long nineteenth century' (1780–1920) through case studies of 'famous' families, including an analysis of gender and age in shaping sibling relationships in the Gladstone family and the deliberate silence surrounding Sigmund Freud's siblings. In so doing, she reveals themes such as gender, power and loss in sibling relation-ships through the life course, as well as pointing to other 'forgotten' relationships such as those with aunts and uncles, nieces and nephews and cousins.

Thus, we see that, even in those disciplines such as psychoanalysis, history and sociology where siblings have been 'forgotten', they still inform some of the key anchor points of these disciplines: the inner emotional world in psychoanalysis, experiences of life in past times in history and the shaping of relational selves in sociology. Further-more, in these disciplines, asking questions about siblings can help to reveal new angles or ways of seeing central themes, revealing other forms of influence and ways of relating.

This chapter explores some of the empirical questions that scholars have asked about siblings, from psychological questions pertaining to the influence of having a brother or sister on childhood development – which dominate academic studies of siblings – to the use of aspects of sibship configuration as a variable in quantitative analyses of educational and occupational outcomes and practice-based questions about how vulnerable siblings can be supported. The chapter then moves on to a discussion of the sorts of sociological questions that have been posed about siblingship, identifying opportunities for new ways of looking both *at* and *with* siblings sociologically.

Asking questions about child development

Psychologists have perhaps asked the most questions about siblings, or at least questions about siblings have been more central to the development of the discipline of psychology than they have been to sociology, history or psychoanalysis. It is not my intention to provide an overview of siblings in psychology here. Rather, I wish to highlight the sorts of questions about siblings that have been typically posed in psychological studies and to explore how examining siblingship has revealed different forms of psychological thinking. Judy Dunn's many works on sibling relationships have been central to psychological understandings of siblings. In her paper outlining the 'state of the art' as she sees it, Dunn identified three domains of interest: 1) 'the potential influence of sisters and brothers on each other's development and adjustment'; 2) the opportunity to provide new perspectives on development issues, 'particularly the "hot topic" of how children come to understand other people's feelings and minds'; and 3) the challenge that studying the 'significance of their shared and separate family experiences and their genetic relatedness' can bring to studies of familial influence on development (Dunn, 2000 [1982]: 244).

These themes are explored by Dunn in her 1985 book, *Sisters and Brothers: The Developing Child*, where she poses questions about the influence of siblings on childhood development and wonders 'Why should some siblings get along so well, and others fight and quarrel with such hostility?' (1985: 1), a question that she also explores with Carol Kendrick (Dunn and Kendrick, 1982) in a longitudinal study of sibling relationships in 40 families following the birth of a second child. In this study Dunn and Kendrick seek to identify factors that enable some families to navigate this first year of multiple children more 'successfully' than others.

These questions, centring on the role of siblings in individual development in childhood, but also considering how the properties of siblinghood – as Dunn saw them in the 1980s – raise broader questions for the discipline, tap into many of the conundrums associated with how siblings turn out that were identified as of popular interest in the previous chapter. Indeed, Dunn explicitly asks: 'why are siblings, who grow up in the same family and share the same parents (and 50 per cent of their genes), nevertheless strikingly different from one another in personality and adjustment?' (2000 [1982]: 244).

Though sociologists might be interested in why these questions prove to be so intriguing, a sociological approach – certainly one in line with current sociological thinking about families, intimacy and relationships – would hopefully help the researcher to recognise diversity in family forms, identifying the assertion that siblings share parents and genes as a normative presumption that obscures different relational features and experiences of sibling relationships. A sociological approach would likely ask different questions, moving away from a focus on individual development and personality to think instead about questions of the socially constituted self, of how sibling relationships might affect our interaction with other social institutions and wider relational forms. Sociology, I think, also helps us to look beyond childhood, using different frames to that of 'development' to help us to conceive of the importance of siblingship through the life course. I also think that a sociological approach to understanding relationships helps maintain a focus on connection and the living, doing and imagining of relationships through time, rather than looking at how a relationship might have an effect on an individual or what formulas can help us to see relationships as 'successful'.

In their more recent (2017) book, Naomi White and Claire Hughes continue to ask questions about the role of siblings in development, this time extending the analysis to focus on the influence of siblings through the life course. White and Hughes cover early childhood and the arrival of new siblings as well as how siblings support one another at school and through disability and chronic illness. The authors also consider the effect of demographic shifts and fertility rates on family form along with a recognition of cultural diversity that updates some of the assumptions made in earlier psychological studies of sibling relationships about genetic relatedness and an imagined nuclear family. Some of these questions hint at more sociological themes of temporality, life course and social change which I return to in Chapter 5. However, White and Hughes's focus remains very much on questions of individual development, a key psychological lens through which to examine relationships and relational forms.

The idea that questions of parenting and genes raise interesting lines of inquiry about nature and nurture is, however, still important, and we see this enacted in the methodological approach of twin studies. The classic twin study methodology was first described by Sir Francis Galton, a London scholar and cousin of Charles Darwin, in two texts: 'The History of Twins as a Criterion of the Relative Powers of Nature and Nurture' published in 1875 and 'Inquiries into Human Faculty and Its Development' published in 1883. In these works, Galton first raised the idea that studying twins could enable scientists to distinguish between the effects of heredity and nurture (Segal, 1999; Stewart, 2000). Dona Lee Davis tracks more recent trends in twin studies which are dominated by the fields of psychology as well as biology and biomedicine and continue to centre around ideas of genetic determinism, the role of DNA as a 'blueprint for self' (2014: 4) where '[e]mphasis is placed on sameness or being the same' (2014: 4). Davis's own work explores the cultural and performative nature of resemblances between twins, unpicking the role of twin studies in creating and perpetuating ideas about twinship. Nancy Segal, a psychologist who has undertaken many twin studies, describes twins as 'Living Laboratories' (1999: 1) and points to the ways that twin studies seem able to home in on those questions about how we come to be the way we are that hold such cultural fascination. Segal writes: 'Aiming the research spotlight on the lives of identical and fraternal twins captures vital clues to solving the behavioural riddles that each of us pose' (1999: xvi).

Though there are many critiques of twin studies and their methodologies, not least the question of how far twins can be said to have shared an environment (see Stewart, 2000, and Segal, 1999, for full discussions), the continued use of twin studies points to the lasting fascination with questions of nature and nurture in scientific inquiry, as well as shaping normative cultural understandings of the role of twins and assumptions about the resemblances between them (Davis, 2014).

Asking questions with siblings as a variable

In twin studies we see twinship employed as a methodology to explore other issues, with twins used to 'control' for variables pertaining to nature and nurture. Siblingship itself is also sometimes used as a variable in quantitative studies in both sociology and psychology. In these works questions are posed about how characteristics of a sibship such as birth-order position, age gap, gender composition, number of siblings and so on can explain various life course outcomes, almost all concerning children or young people. These outcomes tend to pertain to life course transitions and predominantly explore measures of educational achievement such as qualifications, educational routes pursued on leaving compulsory education and test scores in key areas such as literacy, with an underlying assumption that these will influence subsequent occupational opportunities and income. Lala Carr Steelman and colleagues (2002) point to a long history of investigations seeking to identify the effect of having siblings on children's and young people's education. They argue that the study of sibship size broadens sociological understandings of small groups and contributes to debates about the intergenerational transfer of human, economic, social and cultural capital: 'Sibship size has been a staple variable embodied in the status attainment paradigm, predicting status outcomes such as educational attainment, earnings, and occupational attainment' (2002: 246).

Most of the many studies that seek to explore the impact of sibship size on educational outcomes tend to follow a similar understanding of social transmission to James Coleman's (1988) model of social capital transmission, in which siblings are understood to dilute parentally provided capital. Judith Blake (1989), for example, found that children with more siblings were less likely to participate in activities indicative of cultural capital such as extracurricular activities or travel. Dalton Conley (2004) pursues a similar framing, conceiving of a sibship as a 'pecking order' in his analysis of 'which siblings succeed', pointing in particular to the stretching of parentally provided financial assistance to pay for college education, which, he argues, results in parents backing the child they see as most likely to succeed.

Questions about the statistical significance of the configuration of a sibship have also been asked by sociologists and social psychologists. Though seemingly less statistically significant than size of sibship, questions have been posed about which birth-order position is most advantageous or how gender configurations of sibships might affect various outcomes (see Carr Steelman et al., 2002). Brian Powell and Lala Carr Steelman (1993) found, for example, that a large age gap between siblings yielded better educational outcomes, and Daphne Hsiang-Hui Kuo and Robert M. Hauser (1997) found that eldest siblings fared better in education, with outcomes impaired for subsequent children. Conley's (2004) 'pecking order' also placed eldest siblings in the prime position to monopolise resources. These findings have been somewhat contested, and in a later study Powell and Carr Steelman (1995) suggested that younger siblings, rather than accessing a smaller share of parental resources, could benefit from having older, more financially stable parents. The idea that parental resources are not shared equally also runs counter to dominant discourses surrounding the parenting of siblings where there is a moral imperative to treat children equally and avoid 'favouritism' (see Heath, 2018).

Though these theorisations, and the empirical work they have inspired, ask questions – and often questions relating to sociological kinds of concerns such as social structures, inequalities and institutions – where the focus is directly on siblingship, in presuming that siblings essentially share parentally provided social, cultural and economic capital these studies still only explore intergenerational transmission. The use of siblings as a variable, whose effect on various outcomes can be measured, results in a conceptualisation of siblings as passive recipients of parentally provided capital, and the relationship between brothers and sisters, including how they might pass capital between one another, remains underexplored. Throughout this book I return to the idea that we do indeed inherit things from our siblings. This deficit approach to the passing down of capital has been robustly critiqued by childhood sociologists for failing to recognise children's agency as active participants in the transference of capital (see Holland, 2008; Hadfield et al., 2006;

Gillies and Lucey, 2006, for critiques) and I return to some alternative child-centred visions of siblings and social capital later in this chapter.

Asking questions about supporting siblings

The significance of children's sibling relationships in and of themselves has been more central to the work of practitioners working to support vulnerable children and families. The UK's Social Care Institute for Excellence/National Institute for Health and Care Excellence (SCIE/NICE) recommendations on looked-after children contain guidelines about attending to sibling relationships when children and young people are placed in social care. The 2010 report clearly outlines the importance of sibling relationships:

> Evidence suggests that membership of a sibling group is a unique part of the identity of a child or young person and can promote a sense of belonging and promote positive self-esteem and emotional wellbeing. Good management of sibling placement and contact is important to encourage and nurture healthy relationships, and can also help children and young people manage relationships they may find difficult. Siblings can include those who are not looked after and 'sibling-like' relationships that develop in a care setting. (SCIE/NICE, 2010)

The guidelines include a broad definition of siblings which incorporates step-siblings. The acknowledgement of the significance of 'sibling-like' relationships and the attention to the particularities of sibling relationships when making decisions brings a more constructionist and sociological definition of sibling relationships which emphasises children's experiences. There are guidelines concerning the placement of siblings together and, where decisions are made to separate siblings, the guidelines ensure that plans are put in place for continued contact. Social work scholars have noted, for example, that siblings fare better – or at least as well – in care when placed together, and that good reasons must be presented for separating siblings when placing them in social care (Hegar, 2005; Jones, 2016). The centrality of maintaining sibling relationships in adoption, fostering and social care placements is also present in other countries.

For example, in the US the Fostering Connections to Success and Increasing Adoption Act of 2008 similarly mandated that states must make 'reasonable efforts' to place siblings together. Despite this acknowledgement of the importance of sibling relationships, academics have also noted a lack of attention to the role of siblings in debates about child welfare, which have, following the pattern established in other disciplines – including sociology – foregrounded adult–child relationships (McCormik, 2010; Saunders and Selwyn, 2011). This absence is particularly apparent in approaches to sibling relationships that are abusive, harmful or dangerous and that may require interventions from social workers or counsellors. Scholars of counselling and social work have pointed to the difficulties in defining and recognising emotional, physical and sexual abuse between siblings despite its prevalence. Mark S. Kiselica and Mandy Morrill-Richards, writing in the *Journal of Counselling and Development*, argue that '[c]onsidering the pandemic nature of sibling abuse, it is alarming how little has been done to address the issue. Families and society dismiss abuse among brothers and sisters as normal sibling rivalry' (2007: 157).

Kiselica and Morrill-Richards offer a model for counselling families where sibling abuse occurs, pointing to the failure of many parents and guardians to handle abuse appropriately when it is disclosed. Amy Meyers (2014; 2017) similarly indicates a lack of attention to physical and emotional sibling abuse in US social work where there are no consistent laws or legal definitions of sibling abuse, resulting in child protection workers often failing to recognise it and with limited mandates to intervene when abuse is identified. Despite resulting in significant damage to survivors, Meyers describes sibling abuse as existing under a 'veil' (2017: 333), often indistinguishable from other more taken-for-granted forms of sibling conflict. These difficulties in defining and recognising abuse as different from sibling conflict are explored further by Heather Hensman Kettrey and Beth C. Emery, who, in their survey of college students' experiences of sibling violence, found that respondents 'utilized terminology in a manner that failed to recognize their experience as a form of violence' (2006: 407). Ultimately, students were unable to classify their siblings' behaviour as violent due to dominant discourses about the taken-for-granted nature of sibling conflict which renders physical violence between siblings invisible.

These analyses of why sibling abuse often goes unrecognised point to societal norms about the nature of sibling relationships that obscure abuse. Research in this area has also placed sibling abuse within wider family dynamics so that understandings of and responses to sibling abuse incorporate a recognition of the role of conflict between parents in perpetuating problems of sibling violence (Hoffman, Kiecott and Edwards, 2005) and the correlation between sibling abuse and parent–child abuse, child neglect and parental favouritism is noted (Meyers, 2014).

Also considering the importance of orienting sibling support within wider family dynamics, Sarah Meakings, Amanda Coffey and Katherine H. Shelton (2017) explore the complexities of the negotiation of sibling relationships in adoption – attending to the diversity of sibship configurations that are so formed. In so doing, they question how siblings placed in adoptive families together renegotiate their relationships in the context of the wider family, asking how new sibling relationships may be formed while acknowledging that siblings who are not placed together may face a lack in continuation of their relationship. In their analysis of court records and interviews with adoptive parents, Meakings, Coffey and Shelton point to the difficulties experienced by parents in dealing with new sibling relationships and shifts in sibships, urging social workers to attend to the needs of existing children in families where newly adopted children are placed. The authors suggest the implementation of a family systems framework to enable the recognition of the complexities of the multitude of sibling relationships that might be created, curtailed and changed as a result of adoption.

Meakings, Coffey and Shelton found a particular gap in support for existing children in families who have recently adopted new children. Alyson Rees and Andrew Pithouse (2019) also point to the importance of birth children, and they qualitatively explored the experiences of birth children in ten UK foster families. Rees and Pithouse found that the children in their study engaged in 'sibling-like' mediation activities which eventually brought what the authors term an 'indispensable "glue"' to their relationships (2019: 361). By looking at sibling relationships in terms of the practices and processes that create them, these works explore siblingship from a more sociological angle, questioning taken-for-granted generalisations about the structure and experience of sibling relationships.

In addition to the importance of siblings in social work practice and thinking, there is a body of work exploring the experiences of the siblings of disabled children. In some respects this work considers sibling relationships through the lens of a similar deficit or dilution model as the transference of capital discussed above in relation to studies of siblings inspired by Coleman's (1988) model of social capital, where the siblings of disabled children are understood to receive fewer parentally provided resources, particularly financial assets and parents' time and attention (Richardson and Jordan, 2017). Others have also noted that siblings of disabled children often expect to take responsibility for the care of their brother or sister when their parents become old or die (McCaffrey, 2008), or that these sibling relationships might be less close and more conflictual (see Meltzer, 2018, for an overview). However, these works have been criticised by social scientists who attend to the agency of children and who have considered the benefits for children of having a disabled sibling – both in terms of shaping them as a person in positive ways but also because the relationship is important and has merit in and of itself. This attention to the relationship between siblings is more in keeping with other sociological studies of siblingship. In her chapter outlining the work of the UK charity Sibs, which supports people who grow up with a disabled sibling, Monica McCaffrey (2008) points to some of the difficulties experienced by young people who access the charity, including feelings of isolation, ignorance about their sibling's condition, lack of access to parental time, financial difficulties and lack of public awareness. However, she also points to positives, stating, 'There is no question that the experience of having been raised with a disabled brother or sister can deliver real advantages in life' (2008: 103). These advantages are said to include the development of empathy and leadership skills.

Though attending to the agency of children and recognising a more nuanced sibling relationship than those studies outlined above which use siblings as a variable, this approach still considers the sibling relationship in terms of outcomes – what does a person stand to gain or lose from being and having siblings? Ariella Meltzer's Australian study of children with and without siblings moves beyond an engagement with the deficit model, however nuanced, to look at how 'disability is embodied and enacted in: how siblings engage in supportive and conflictual talk and everyday chat with each other;

how they enact recreation and seek connection with each other; and how they strive to understand and experience their emotions about each other' (2018: 1212). In posing these questions, Meltzer explores the complexities and ups and downs of siblingship in the context of disability by placing the relationship itself at the centre of her analysis. In this way, Meltzer also accounts for disabled children's experiences of being and having siblings and does not focus only on how their disability might affect non-disabled siblings.

Taken together, these studies point to the significance of sibling relationships in children's lives, acknowledging the importance of contact between siblings and the effects that living with another child can have, as well as emphasising the experience of the relationship itself.

Asking sociological questions about siblings

Despite existing largely on the periphery of studies about family, kinship or social networks, there is a small but growing sociology of sibling relationships. These works, mainly but not exclusively rooted in childhood studies, qualitatively address the experience of being and having siblings, highlighting the social construction of siblingship and pointing to the negotiation of gender and birth order within sibships and the creation of siblingship through practices. In their analysis of sibling relationships in middle childhood, Ros Edwards and colleagues (2006) combine social constructionist and psychodynamic perspectives to explore issues of identity and relationality, which they place at the heart of sibling relationships. The social constructionist aspect of their analysis has resulted in a conceptualisation of the meanings and realities of being/having a sibling as multiple, negotiated and continuously shifting, and the psychoanalytical influence on their work ensures that they remain mindful of the emotional impact of siblingship. Here the authors borrow concepts from psychoanalysis such as 'projection' to explain how siblings influence one another's identity, and the role of fear and anxiety in the conflictual desire to be both an individual and part of a group, which the authors see as central to siblingship. The incorporation of a poststructuralist attention to discourse also means that, although fluid and contextual, sibling relationships are still understood as influenced by underlying social structures, and the authors maintain that '[c]hildren and young people are both subject to predominant discourses and structures of, and creators of the lived social practices of, age, class, ethnicity, gender and so on' (Edwards et al., 2006: 10).

Melanie Mauthner's (2005a; 2005b) work on sistering applies similar frames, asking questions about the influence of sibling relationships on the ways gender identity is formed through the life course, exploring caring and power relations among sisters while also asking questions about the changing subjectivities, conscious and unconscious thoughts and emotions that Mauthner sees as central to the sister relationships she studies. Thus, Mauthner explores the social construction of sistering and attends to the external circumstances, structures and power dynamics that shape sister relationships, along with what she terms the 'internal shifts' in sisters' fluctuating power and subjectivities (2005b). Along with Edwards and colleagues (2006), Mauthner sees siblinghood as central to the relationship between self and society, arguing that 'tensions within sistering can illuminate our understanding of the interaction between subject and society, in this case between an autonomous self and one embedded in family networks' (2005b: 176).

Indeed, questions about how sibling relationships inform self and identity have been a fruitful focus of inquiry for those sociologists who have attended to siblingship, and the following chapter picks up and extends some of these debates. Edwards and colleagues point to the centrality of sameness and difference in the language of siblingship and the effect of this on how young people construct their own sense of self. They write:

> Sameness and difference, then, are two of the key intersubjective notions that children and young people use when describing and reflecting upon their own sense of self, notions that are closely tied up with feelings about individuality and being part of a group, belonging, connection and separation, dependence and independence. (2006: 38)

Miri Song's work on mixed-race siblings (2010) builds upon issues of sameness and difference by taking account of the interaction between cultural identity and identification between mixed-race siblings. Song attends to interactions between choice and constraint in the construction of ethnic identity, and points to how siblings are constructed as ethnically different within family scripts of ethnicity due to identifying features such as their friends, cultural taste and appearance, highlighting similar themes of colourism to those fictionalised by Andrea Levy in her 1996 novel *Never Far from Nowhere*. The importance of physical appearance (particularly differences in skin colour between siblings) to some families in Song's research highlights the significance of family resemblances – or differences – between siblings and demonstrates the importance of embodiment, race, ethnicity and culture to the development of the relational self within families.

Similar questions about the role of physical resemblance in the construction of identity are posed by Kate Bacon (2012) in her sociological exploration of the meaning of twinship. Looking at twins from a sociological perspective enables Bacon to consider children's and young people's understandings of what being a twin means to them, moving beyond the 'twins as a research method' approach so widely deployed in psychological studies. Bacon explores the complexities of agency and interdependency in the lives of twins who are constructing themselves as '[b]eings in their own right' (2012: 307) against a backdrop of expectations and realities of physical resemblance. Elizabeth Stewart (2000) also explores twinship sociologically, analysing popular assumptions, myths and misunderstandings about twinship, along with the assumptions of resemblance at the heart of twin studies, as social constructions which shape the world of twins and their families.

Also deeply rooted in social constructionist frameworks, which enable taken-for-granted categories of relationships to be unpicked sociologically, Samantha Punch explores the constructions of birth order within sibling groups, arguing that birth-order roles 'are not fixed hierarchies but can be subverted, contested, resisted and negotiated through children's everyday experiences of family life' (2008: 30). In an earlier paper Punch (2005) drew on Erving Goffman (1959) to illustrate how sibling relationships tend to be more 'backstage' than parent–child relationships, largely because they are seen to be less characterised by fixed, generational power differentials and thus require a less careful presentation of self.

Focusing particularly (though not exclusively) on child siblings in Denmark whose families have experienced divorce or separation, Ida Wentzel Winther, Charlotte Palludan, Eva Gulløv and Mads

Middelboe Rehder (2015a) ask questions about the construction and negotiation of sibling relationships in the context of divorce. Using qualitative interviews, dialogues between siblings and filmed observations, the authors tap into the everyday lives of siblings, asking child-centred questions about the meaning of siblingship and 'how material, social and cultural contexts influence the way siblingship is performed and perceived' (2015a: 9). Wentzel Winther and colleagues sensitively handle the complexities of birth order and age gap, using Davidoff's (2012) differentiation between long and wide siblingships and short and narrow siblingships to differentiate between 'long' relationships with large age gaps, 'wide' sibships where children have different parents and are spread across different households, and 'short' and 'narrow' relationships where children are closer in age and live together in the same households. The authors move far away from comparing the 'outcomes' of these different sibling groups and instead ask questions about how these relationships are given meaning through the everyday practices, performances and experiences of siblings. The film that the authors made to accompany their written findings (Wentzel Winther et al., 2015b) demonstrates the importance of this focus on the everyday, highlighting the role of material and embodied aspects of siblingship, including the meaning of home and time spent in the spaces in between homes while taking journeys between parents' homes together.

Similarly focusing on children's siblingship, Hayley Davies's book on children's lives and relationships contains a chapter devoted to siblings. Davies highlights the ways siblingship is practised in the everyday, pointing to the embodied and sensory nature of siblingship as well as looking sociologically at the emotional ups and downs of siblingship. Davies uses concepts from sociology and geography to understand how 'proximity and close contact facilitate and shape children's relationships' (2015: 66). I go on to discuss this in more detail in Chapter 3.

These sociological studies all pose questions about the meanings of sibling relationships and what it is like to have siblings – questions about sibling relationships in their own right without a need to use siblings to explain other seemingly more 'worthy' topics such as educational attainment. However, a handful of sociology studies do consider the benefits of being or having siblings for aspects of society that are perhaps seen as more central to the discipline of sociology, such as education, health or housing. These approaches often consider siblingship through the lens of social capital or social networks, offering a significant counter to Coleman's (1988) 'dilution' model of the effect of sibship size on access to social capital. Janet Holland, for example, discusses how older siblings (and other relatives) already in school can provide valuable 'insider information' (2008: 12) about school as well as emotional support and a 'bridge' to the formation of new friendships. Lucy Hadfield and colleagues also show how older siblings can provide a source of support for young people who are experiencing bullying at school, demonstrating how, although some siblings were found to relish the space away from a sibling that school provided, siblings would always step in to offer support against bullies, regardless of the quality of the sibling relationship (2006: 68). Similarly, Val Gillies and Helen Lucey found that '[e]ven where sibling relationships were conflictual and strained brothers and sisters were broadly acknowledged to be an important source of knowledge and experience' (2006: 490). More recently, Sanna Aaltonen (2016) has pointed to how siblings provide knowledge about educational decision making in Finland. By theorising children as agentic actors and attending to their accounts and experiences of being and having siblings, these sociological studies have emphasised potential benefits of siblingship in a way that challenges assumptions about the intergenerational transmission of social capital.

Asking questions about cultural diversity

Despite the importance of considering how siblingship is shaped by cultural, ethnic and racial diversity, there is very little sociological research in which questions about cultural diversity and sibingship have been posed. Miri Song's (2010) research on mixed-race siblings stands out, as Song asks questions about how sibling relationships are constructed in mixed-race families, and in doing so is able to consider questions about the construction of ethnic identity and its interactions with cultural, embodied and relational factors. Loretta Baldassar and Rosa Brandhorst (2021) ask questions about the exchange of care and support between siblings in transnational and migrant families, pointing to a preoccupation in migration literatures with intergenerational exchanges of care across borders. However, lack of empirical research on cultural and ethnic diversity in sibling relationships means it remains very difficult to draw conclusions about the particularities of siblingship as experienced in different ethnic groups.

Research on family relationships in families of different ethnic origin more generally provides clues as to how sibling relationships might be differently experienced. Rich sociological work highlighting the gendered nature of many South Asian family structures, for example, helps us piece together how boys and girls may be treated differently in these contexts. Alison Shaw (2000) and Kalwant Bhopal (1997) both draw out the ways South Asian women are often conduits of the family's reputation in terms of honour and prestige. Michela Franceschelli and Margaret O'Brien's analysis of the ways young Muslims in England navigate their habitus in Islamic and non-Islamic fields emphasises gendered expectations of protection and control in many South Asian families. They write:

> Whether parental control and protection were exercised on both boys and girls, they appeared to affect them differently. Parental gendered expectations perceive young women as the 'guardians' of the family's religious and cultural identity ... Boys instead are seen as the future providers and therefore are granted more freedom and independence. (2015: 708)

Naomi White and Claire Hughes (2018), in their psychological work on siblings and child development, also point to gendered sibling relationships in many South Asian families, where they found that brothers were expected to provide material support for their adult sisters who, in turn, were expected to provide affection and hospitality.

Franceschelli's (2016) analysis of English Muslim young people's transitions to adulthood demonstrates some of the challenges young English Muslims encountered in navigating parental and other intergenerational expectations alongside British cultural norms. This analysis invites questions about the role of siblings – as intra-generational relationships that are more peer-like and that share the challenges of navigating different cultural terrains – in making these transitions.

Anthropologists, asking questions about kinship in the majority world, have drawn attention to different meanings, constructions and practices of siblingship in these diverse contexts. Janet Carsten (1997), for example, identified the unique role of identity and resemblance in siblingship in a Malay fishing community where siblings were representatives of kinship itself, as separate bodies emanating from one body. White and Hughes (2018), in reviewing literature on cultural diversity in sibling relationships, draw attention to religious and cultural rituals where siblings have a particular role. For example, they report that, during the Hindu festival of Raksha Bandhen, sisters traditionally tie an amulet or thread on the wrist of their brothers, praying for their well-being, while brothers vow to protect and provide for their sisters. Mary Chamberlain's (1999, 2006) work on Caribbean families also points to different definitions of siblingship in communities in both the Caribbean and the UK, where sibling terms ('sister' and 'brother') were used to describe relationships with cousins, friends and community, aiding solidarity against racism. Alison Shaw similarly points to the 'playing down' (2000: 95) of biological relatedness in family structures in rural Pakistan, where kin terms for cousins, aunts, brothers and sisters can be used interchangeably in the context of a more collective imagining of the domestic unit.

Victor Cicirelli (1994) explores anthropological work on siblingship to differentiate between siblings in what he terms 'industrialized' and 'non-industrialized' cultures. Cicirelli points to differences in the definition of siblingship as well as in expectations of care, and he found that, in general, greater importance is attached to the role of older siblings as caretakers in non-industrialised societies. Samantha Punch (2004) considers the role of chores and birth order in the negotiation of autonomy among children in rural Bolivia. Ruth Evans (2011) also points to the significance of sibling relationships in caringscapes among youth-headed households affected by AIDS in Uganda and Tanzania. It is important, however, not to ask questions that overly generalise cultural differences. Dowries, for example – as explained by White and Hughes (2018) – are certainly not used by all South Asian families, and Cicirelli's distinction between industrialised and non-industrialised countries, though a helpful reminder that siblingship must be understood beyond the minority world, is so broad as to conceal as much diversity as it illuminates. What these works can indicate, however, is that the ways that sibling roles, identities and relationships are practised, understood and imagined are culturally diverse, and more research is needed that asks sociological questions about the lived experience of siblingship in different cultural contexts.

The interviews and focus groups in this book engage young people from a diverse range of backgrounds, and I point to these diversities when possible, as well as drawing on examples from beyond these contexts. Information about the ethnicity of mass observers is not always available unless the writers themselves draw attention to this in their account. It has not been possible, therefore, to make generalisations about how siblingship might be experienced differently by different ethnic groups from the data presented in this volume, and more research is desperately needed in this area. Sociological questions about diversity must be able to explore the particularities of the experiences of different groups in an intersectional way that explores the dynamics of gender, class and place as well as ethnic and racial diversity.

Conclusion

This chapter has pointed to some of the questions that scholars have asked about siblings, from questions posed by psychologists about the role of siblings in shaping child development, to the use of twins to answer questions about 'nature versus nurture' and the use of sibship configurations as a variable to be correlated with educational and occupational outcomes. I have also pointed to more sociologically oriented work that asks practice-based questions about how best to care for and support siblings, before attending to explicitly sociological points of departure in work that explores sibling relationships in terms of identity, social constructionism and social capital. In unpacking what thinking sociologically about siblingship can bring to our understandings, I do not seek to dismiss non-sociological approaches, but instead to build on them in various ways. I also go on to extend the sociology of siblings into different fields of sociological inquiry. In Chapter 3 I continue to ask questions about care and support for siblings, setting these against the discursive significance of the relationship between aspects of the sibship such as birth order, age, gender and sibship size, and 'outcomes' such as educational achievement in the popular imagination. Drawing on sociological work which unpicks how the psy-sciences work to create the self in late modernity, in Chapter 2 I ask questions about what it means to grow up with siblings, who are understood as being central to development. My theoretical framework for the forthcoming chapters is also heavily influenced by the anthropological focus on kin networks and the role of genetics and biology in shaping these, and I consider the social construction of sibling relationships in ways that account for aspects of siblingship that might be considered beyond the reach of traditional sociological inquiry such as emotions and sensory, embodied and ethereal connections. In so doing the book extends existing questions about siblings as well as asking new questions about the role of key sociological ideas about self, relationality, imagination and temporality in shaping our sibling relationships, explaining why sibling relationships are so important.

But more than that I also consider how we can think sociologically *with* siblings. Throughout the chapters that follow I use elements of what makes siblings intriguing and important to ask bigger questions about how we might reimagine central features of sociological thought. I use the complexities and ambivalences at the heart of many sibling relationships: the paradox of being an individual while being inextricably linked to one's siblings through comparison, resemblance and generational proximity; the disconnect between normative ideals and imagined siblings and the 'real life' complexities of lived sibling relationships; the magical, ethereal and uncanny connections that siblings may experience; the apparent paradox of 'being there' for a sibling while also physically fighting or avoiding each other in certain social contexts; and the ways sibling relationships ebb and flow through the life course. I put these ideas to work to explore how these intricacies help us to see new things and ask different questions about the social construction of the self, what it means to be related, how normativity, morality and imagination intertwine with lived experience, and about the interactions of different temporal registers (everyday proximities, shared memory, ideas of the future, transition and critical moments).

Chapter 2

Self

Being a sibling can have a profound effect on our identity and sense of self, and in this chapter I explore how sibling relationships can influence our sense of who we are and what we can become in the future. The following discussion addresses how being a sibling implicates both self (understood as a process of self-identification – our own sense of who we are, formed in relation to others) and identity (understood as a form of categorisation – how others see us) (Jenkins, 2004). Being a sibling means being one in a series, with individuality often constructed in relation to the sibship as a whole (Edwards et al., 2006) through the comparing of siblings. Focusing upon what is similar and different about siblings encourages others to conceptualise them in relation to one another. These comparisons are particularly likely to be made by parents, teachers, relatives, friends and neighbours who have a long-term knowledge of the siblings as children, as well as by siblings themselves. However, we do not have to possess an intimate knowledge of siblings to be interested in their similarities and differences. As we saw in the introduction, the fascination with how siblings who have grown up in the same home and share genetic heritage can often turn out to be different is often utilised in fictional accounts of sibling relationships, from Bart and Lisa Simpson to the sisters in Jane Austen's *Sense and Sensibility*, where differences in talents, character, personality, humour and so on are used as a central narrative device. Furthermore, we have seen that siblings are often heralded as a fitting test case for thinking through the formation of the self, with the identification of similarities and differences between siblings prompting debates about nature versus nurture: did tennis superstars Venus and Serena Williams's talent for tennis come from genetics or from their upbringing with their tennis coach father? How can 'long-lost' siblings, reunited after being brought up separately, discover commonalities – not just in physical appearance or health, but also in tastes, humour or outlook? My intention here is not to come up with answers to these questions, but rather to frame the account of how being and having siblings can implicate our sense of self within a context of wider public and cultural interest in these issues.

Sociologists have had a long-term interest in the social construction of the self, with accounts by sociologists such as George Herbert Mead (1934), Ian Burkitt (2008) and Richard Jenkins (2004) emphasising the self and social identity as constructed in relation to significant others. These ideas about the relational nature of the self are now a fundamental part of the discipline. However, sociological theorising about the formation of the self has tended to focus intergenerationally on the role of parents in shaping who we are and who we can become in the future. Think, for example, of Mead's theory of the formation of the relational self and Pierre Bourdieu's (1990) thesis on the inculcation of habitus, both of which have influenced much sociological thinking today, and imply that the traits, tendencies and characteristics that make up the self largely pass *downwards* in the family, with parents seen as crucial in both accounts. An exception is James S. Coleman's (1988) work on social capital, where the presence of siblings is explicitly acknowledged. However, Coleman still sees parents as central to the transmission of capital, and as such he argues that, rather than actively providing capital themselves, the presence of siblings dilutes parentally provided capital. This argument has been robustly critiqued by sociologists of childhood who have pointed to children as active agents in the transmission of capital (see Holland, 2008; Hadfield et al., 2006; Gillies and Lucey, 2006). In this chapter I explore the important role of siblings in shaping the self, arguing that it is precisely because of the lateral nature of sibling relationships that they can affect our sense of self and identity so profoundly.

This chapter begins with an extended discussion of two sisters, Anna and Francesca, who both took part in interviews after I advertised the research at Romsbridge, the school Francesca attended. This in-depth analysis of the sisters' different stories and perspectives enables the narratives of similarity and difference in Anna and Francesca's relationship to be unpacked, demonstrating how these processes shape the sisters' ideas about the people they are, their understandings of their experiences of school and their sense of their future. The remainder of the chapter discusses some of the key themes involved in the relationship between siblings and the self, outlining how sibling identity is relationally constructed through a discussion of the comparing of siblings and the application of relational labels concerning character and appearance. A paradox between the relational construction of sibling identity and Western ideals of authentic personhood is identified. The chapter then moves on to discuss the role of others in the relational construction of sibling identity through an exploration of how they are shaped through the telling of family stories. The chapter concludes with a discussion of how identity can be informed by a sibling's reputation in and between different contexts such as school, home or community.

Anna and Francesca: a story of two sisters

Anna and Francesca are sisters – I interviewed them separately in their home in 2007 after Francesca brought a leaflet about the study home from school. Francesca was 12 years old and in her second year at Romsbridge (their local school). Anna was 14 years old and in her fourth year at a different school. The girls described being given a degree of choice of school, with Anna choosing her school because of its 'good' reputation, and Francesca opting for the local school because it was more familiar and her friends from primary school attended it. Anna and Francesca's parents are divorced and at the time of the interviews they were living with their mother (a nurse) in a small terraced house. Their mother's mother lived locally and they saw a lot of her. Their father also lived locally with his partner and their two children (Anna and Francesca's half-siblings). Their mother is white British and they described their father as 'half Italian or half Brazilian'. The girls were not entirely sure what their father did for a living, but they thought it was 'something like a lawyer or solicitor'.

Anna and Francesca have similar dark hair and eyes, though Anna's hair is curly and Francesca's straight. They described themselves in terms of their differences, and a narrative of the sisters as 'opposites' had arisen, perpetuated by others in the wider family such as their mother and grandmother. Anna was seen as 'confident', 'loud' and 'outgoing' with Francesca as 'quiet'. A key concern for both sisters in their interviews was the difference between their experiences of school, with Anna enjoying her social and academic life and Francesca struggling to 'settle', experiencing difficulties making friends and being teased by some older children (Anna described this as bullying though Francesca did not use this word). At the time of the interviews various members of the family were involved in discussions about whether it would be better for Francesca to move schools.

Francesca and Anna's conceptualisations of how they see themselves as 'turning out' at school were compounded by the perceptions of the differences between them, and their experiences of school were compared and constructed in opposition. Francesca's perception of her failure to settle in at school was informed by Anna's school experiences, despite them attending different schools, and Francesca (and others in the family) used Anna's experiences as a benchmark by which her own experiences were measured. Francesca's unhappiness at school was viewed *in relation* to Anna's experience (of settling well after a short period of challenge in Year 7 – the first year of secondary education in the UK) and, in Francesca's interpretation at least, she is not measuring up:

> Francesca: My dad, erm, says, 'You're going to be in that school for, like, years, so you really should move', erm, 'if you, like, not settling in', but erm, my mum on the other hand doesn't really want me to move schools and says, I'll, erm, cos my mum and dad don't live together, she says that, 'This is how it was with Anna in Year 7' and, and, like, and 'when she first came to a new school', but the thing is, Anna, Anna settled in at, like, the end of Year 7 and I've still not, it's just like.

In addition to Anna's very different experience of school being used as a benchmark against which Francesca's experience was evaluated (comparisons that informed the families' decision-making process about whether Francesca should move schools), these differences also informed Anna and Francesca's conceptualisations of the very nature of the self, limiting their sense of the possibilities of change. Anna in particular lived by the idea of a fixed, 'true' essential self which she used to draw comparisons between her and

Francesca's school identity, and which reinforced her presentation of herself as *naturally* outgoing and popular and Francesca conversely as *properly* 'geeky':

> Anna: She's a proper geek and everyone knows it. Like, my mum's, my mum, like, cos she's been bullied and everything at school, so she finds it quite hard whereas I'm, like, all right. But *she hasn't got a backbone like I have*, cos I stick up for myself and she doesn't, so she's, she just stays in the corner, whereas I would say something, but she's not, she's not like that. [my emphasis]

When considering the possible reasons for this difference in experience, Anna talks about absolute, fixed differences in character between her and her sister, drawing on the embodied metaphor of the possession (or not) of a 'backbone' to emphasise this point. In the quote below Anna further emphasises the essential nature of these differences by describing herself as always being that way:

> Anna: I don't know. I think I was always more of the, I think it's cos I'm just louder than her and she's, like. And because, er, I think it's the fact that I had friends, like, good, I've always been a dead outgoing person so every single weekend, Friday, Saturday, Sunday, I'm out, I'm never in the house and she's never out. She's always in with my mum and, like, my mum, her and my nana, are dead close. Whereas I'm not really into all that, so. I'm more of, like, 'let's go out and party'. And she's like, 'let's stay in and read a book', so.

These narratives of fundamentally opposite essential characteristics implicate Anna and Francesca's sense of their academic abilities and future potential. Anna, for example, is considered (particularly by their grandmother) to be the 'clever one'. Although Anna never described herself as more intelligent than her sister in her interview (perhaps this would contradict the narrative she created of being popular and fun-loving), she did seem to feel the pressure to achieve that accompanied her grandmother's label of 'intelligent':

> Interviewer: Yeah. Do you ever, like, worry about not doing well at school?
>
> Anna: Yeah … Like, I got a C in ICT [Information and Communication Technology] the other day and I never fretted so much in my life. So I stayed after school and did, like, an hour revision, to help my, like, boost my level back up. [overlapping]

Interviewer: Did you? So, what's, is your fear just, kind of, erm, not doing very well or do you worry that you'll come home and you'll get told off or something, or? [overlapping]

Anna: Oh, I'm always getting told off, that doesn't bother me. I'm just, it, like, if I don't do well, the thing is, like, my nana, like I said, 'Oh, yeah, I got a B the other day in Maths', and she's like, 'Well, why didn't you get an A?', things like that, are just, like.

Interviewer: High expectations. [laughs] [overlapping]

Anna: Yeah. That's, she is, she has loads, and if I say anything, she's like, 'Yeah, well why didn't you get?' and I'm just like, 'Oh, right, okay', like. But my mum's, like, 'Oh, well done, well done', so I'm, like, I don't mind. But I just try, I try hardest and I feel like, to, like, I want to go home to, home to my nana and be like, 'Yeah, I got really good things', so she's happy.

Francesca mentioned Anna's superior intelligence a number of times in her interview as well as referring to her own lack of intelligence. Francesca seems to have accepted unquestioningly her position as less clever than her sister:

Interviewer: ... so do you think you might go to university and stuff when you leave school or...?

Francesca: I'm not very bright for university, so, erm, but...

Interviewer: [overlapping] Is that, like, your opinion or have other people said that?

Francesca: My grandma. [laughs]

Interviewer: Right. Do you believe her or do you...?

Francesca: Erm, I don't know, because I really want to graduate. It'll be great to graduate something. But, I kind of do, cos I know I'm not perfect and, I know you've got to be quite brainy for university, I think, I don't know, I would have thought you do, but erm...?

Interviewer: You don't have to be super brainy for university.

Francesca: No, but, like, I know there's no use going to university and being proper dumb and then, you know.

...

Interviewer: Does your, erm, grandma say the same things to your sister?

Francesca: No. It's, Anna, erm, grandma knows that Anna's quite brainy. Like, well, actually I've never heard her say that. [overlapping]

Francesca has really taken on board the idea of Anna's superior intelligence and seems to accept it unquestioningly (despite her grandmother having never said this out loud). Ultimately, Francesca's self (including how she assesses her own intelligence) is constructed in terms of differences from Anna. This means there can only be a 'clever *one*'. In the extract below Francesca is trying to make sense of where this difference comes from:

> Interviewer: Er, erm, have you got any theories on whether, like, how you are at school can run in families, or not?
>
> Francesca: Er, erm, well, I've got, I don't, I don't really know, to be honest, because my sister has got both of the families', erm, intelligence, because my mum's, erm, quite intelligent and my grandma is. But she's [her grandma] not very good at spelling, so I think I take after her a bit. But, erm, my dad, is, he's, he's like, I think, a lawyer, or like, some solicitor, or something. And so, I think my sister, like, takes after him cos he's quite brainy.

It is clear that the relational construction of Francesca as 'not very bright for university' is embedded in a wider web of relationships and relatedness that spans beyond the sisters, implicating the contexts of both home and school. Indeed, the way that Anna and Francesca are seen as turning out is relationally constructed, but this is about more than the sisters comparing themselves to each other. They are part of a web of resemblance narratives within the family and their identities are constructed against an array of narratives of familial similarities and differences. There is a politics to how these resemblances are 'done' and how they are taken on board to inform Anna and Francesca's understandings of who they are and who they might become, and there are inequalities in who has the power to create or challenge narratives of similarity and difference in the family. Francesca, for example, is said to take after her father (by both Anna and her mother) for largely negative reasons. The father is described by both sisters as a difficult character and is unlikely to be viewed as having many positive characteristics by those who liken him to Francesca – Anna (who has argued with him and is currently banned from his house) and her mother (who is divorced from him) – and Francesca seems to accept that these similarities exist (although she is not happy about them). Thus, Francesca's sense of who she is is constructed in relation to her differences from

Anna, but these differences are also constructed in relation to and by others in the family:

[Having been asked what her mum is like]

Francesca: Mmm. I can't explain that, because, erm, she [her mum] says I take after my dad.

Interviewer: Does she? In what way do you think she thinks you take after your dad?

Francesca: Erm, slobbiness ... And, erm, when I get angry ... Erm, cos my dad's a bit angry. Erm, erm, but, I don't, I don't have any of my mum's looks either, but I, kind of, a, we're both, like, different...

...

Interviewer: So do you think that you take after your dad then?

Francesca: Yeah. Well, I don't, I don't know, cos I don't like it when my mum says that.

Interviewer: How come?

Francesca: I don't really like my dad.

In this exchange we get a sense of Francesca as something of a victim in this resemblance narrative; she does not want to take after her father, but she does not seem able to counter this, especially because she also looks like him.

Anna, on the other hand, created some of her own resemblance narratives in the interview and used resemblances as a way of distancing herself from Francesca, which she did by emphasising the similarities between herself and her younger half-sister, focusing particularly on those characteristics (such as loudness) that Francesca is seen to be lacking:

Anna [having talked about not getting along with Francesca]: Whereas my dad, he has a daughter and she's exactly like me, and we're like, best friends. But she's six, but she acts like a 21-year-old. She's so old for her age ... So me and her, like, go around, like, proper, like. She's, she's a loud girl, she's, she's ...

By likening herself to her half-sister, Anna is bringing her half-sister closer in terms of resemblances in ways of being (particularly by pointing out characteristics that they share and that Francesca lacks, such as loudness) and in age (saying she seems much older than she is). As a consequence of bringing her half-sister closer in these ways she is distancing herself from Francesca. Though it is difficult to believe that Anna has an equal friendship with her 6-year-old half-sister, by *telling* the narrative in such a way she is able to use the unlikelihood of this closeness to distance herself further from Francesca.

This example has indicated some of the complexities of how siblingship implicates the self. The oppositional construction of Anna and Francesca's identities takes place within a web of relationships, with their mother, grandmother and father all playing a role. This identity construction has implications for how the sisters evaluate their own experiences of school, with Francesca's concerns about failing to settle amplified by the fact that Anna had settled by that stage in her school career. Furthermore, these relational constructions implicate how the possibilities of the self itself are understood, with the oppositional binaries of the 'clever one' versus the less academic one and the 'loud one' versus the 'quiet one' implicating a sense of a fixed, natural, true inner self bound up in the inheritance of physical and personality-based characteristics.

It is clear that there is a comparability to being a sibling which implicates the construction of the self. In this chapter I unpack the role of others in the creation of these narratives of similarity and difference, pointing to the paradoxical understandings of the self. This paradox is caused by the serial nature of identity as constructed in relation to a sibling, which exists alongside an understanding of an essential fixed self that is somehow of the natural world. The example of Anna and Francesca has also illuminated some of the emotional implications of comparability, and I return to these, along with a discussion of the relational and emotional implications of resemblance, in the following chapter. Here the focus remains on how these aspects of siblingship implicate the construction of self/ identity as a sibling. Thus, the chapter contributes to the plethora of sociological understandings of the relational self.

The relational construction of sibling identity

As the case of Anna and Francesca shows, comparison is a central facet of how siblingship is *done*, by siblings themselves as well as others, particularly parents and teachers. The practice of comparing means that identity is constructed relationally, in relation to how people are similar to or different from others in their sibship. In this section I explore how this relational construction works, from the ways comparisons are made and lived to the implications for self and personhood of being one in a series of siblings.

We often compare ourselves to our siblings, and our ideas about who we are and who we can become in the future are often formed in relation to our sibling(s). Many mass observers compared themselves to their brothers and sisters in the ways they had 'turned out' in life, reflecting on what was similar and different about their temperaments, jobs and lives. E5014, for example, a 46-year-old man, describes the differences in character and sociability between him and his brother (who is three years younger):

> He and I have completely different personalities; he being almost obsessively happy with his own company (having only one or two friends and not desiring any more), whereas although I wouldn't consider myself gregarious I do enjoy socialising and don't fear social situations where I might meet new people.

D1602, a 70-year-old man, similarly emphasised differences between himself and his older brother in character, talents and appearance, citing his brother's temper, more studious nature and 'sportiness' as key differences. Both these observers identified childhood differences that have gone on to shape how they see themselves and their brothers as men.

When asked to describe themselves and their siblings (in terms of traits, tendencies, talents, appearance and so on), most young people I interviewed recited numerous ways in which they were similar to or different from their siblings in terms of 'personality', appearance and education, many drawing upon similar themes to the mass observers above. Many respondents compared themselves to their siblings without being prompted to do so, but what is striking about those who were specifically asked to make comparisons is that most required little or no time to consider their response. It was clear that these young people were drawing on existing, well-rehearsed narratives of similarity and difference. Take the following examples:

Olivia: Well, the two twins, Matthew and Kevin, Matthew's like me, but Kevin is really like Jonathan. They, he goes off in strops, he had a really bad tantrum today.

Richard: I'm similar to my sister but not to my brother. My brother's more like hyperactive...

Reece: I think I'm the same, well my sister loves sport as well and I like sport and she's ... like pretty loud and confident and I'm loud and confident.

These narratives of similarity and difference between siblings are an important part of the environment in which siblings are raised. Older siblings are usually parents' main frame of reference when making sense of their children's development, so it is unsurprising that parents often find themselves comparing pregnancies, births, infant sleep and feeding patterns, experiences of nursery or school and so on. Comparisons can also be heightened beyond the family in the context of school where, even when siblings, like Anna and Francesca, do not attend the same school at the same time, their sibling relationships carry over into school through their knowledge of a sibling's experience. Indeed, growing up in the same familial generation, often in the same household, can make siblings a foil – a comparison and accounting tool – for young people when considering their progress at school, and watching an older sibling advance though the education system can provide a unique insight into a young person's own educational journey (see Davies, 2019, for a full discussion). We saw this clearly in the way Francesca's timescale for settling in to her secondary school was constructed in relation to that of her sister – for Francesca as well as in the reckonings of her mother, father and grandmother. Among those young people who took part in the wider study who did attend the same school as their siblings, it was common to feel as though teachers also measured their behaviour, abilities and progress against that of their brothers and sisters.

Take the following examples:

Tom: Some of the teachers who've teached [*sic*] my sister throughout the whole years say 'Why can't you just be like your sister?' Cos she never talks or whatever and I'm always talking and you just get annoyed and they try and make me the same as my sister.

Kyle: My brother's not that good at school so they [the teachers] thought that I wouldn't be that good either but I actually am.

Farhana: I think they [the teachers] tended like, 'Oh your older sister was like a lot chatty you know you seem quite quiet.'

These comparisons by parents, teachers and young people themselves can cause feelings of anxiety and pressure, and many young people spoke of feeling under pressure to perform as well as their siblings at school. As 12-year-old Ethan states, 'both my brothers have been head boy, and they've got like the best marks in the year ... so I'm pretty, like, got loads of pressure on me'. In the following focus group discussion between young people aged between 13 and 14, Tom describes the pressures and anxieties he experiences as a result of having a 'clever' older sister:

Tom: I think I'm never gonna be as clever as my sister but I don't want my mum and dad to like, you know, think I should erm ... what's the word?

Sofia: You're not good enough?

Tom: Yeah think I'm not good enough and like try and make me as good as her when I know I can't so it's annoying really. It scares me when I see all the work she's doing, I think 'I've got to do that one day'. It's annoying.

In their discussion of sibling identity and relationships in middle childhood, Ros Edwards and colleagues also point to the ways children in their study compared themselves to their brothers and sisters, commenting that sameness and difference 'is the language often used to think about and express significant questions of connection with others' (2006: 38). Though not all siblings are close in age, being of the same generation means that siblings often experience more readily comparable education systems, job markets and cultural signifiers than, say, children and their parents, so it can be useful for these actors to look across a generation and make comparisons. This comparing is encouraged by the fact that siblings often reach developmental and educational milestones in quick succession and, for parents in particular, their other children are likely to be their main points of reference when thinking about how a particular child is turning out. Here I suggest that the lateral nature of siblingship invites and intensifies such comparisons.

Ian McIntosh and Samantha Punch (2009) are critical of the use of the word 'lateral' to describe sibling relationships because it implies an equality that ignores power differentials between siblings. Indeed, though I do find the term 'lateral' useful in making sense of why siblings are particularly comparable, it is clear that there are power dimensions to how these comparisons work, with older siblings more likely to be a benchmark by which younger siblings are measured (with both positive and negative consequences). Interpersonal family politics also implicate power within sibling relationships, and we saw this in the ways Francesca was likened to her father by her mother, grandmother and sister. Other researchers have pointed to the gendered power differentials between siblings in many South Asian families. Alison Shaw (2000), for example, highlights gendered power structures in British Pakistani families and notes the differential treatment of boys and girls due to the gendered nature of *izzat* (honour). Kalwant Bhopal's exploration of dowries in South Asian families highlights the role of women as 'important instruments in the competition for prestige' (1997: 486), emphasising South Asian women's experience of private patriarchy, 'based on household structure as the main site of women's oppression' (1997: 491). Further research into the intersectional nature of sibling power dynamics is vital.

Within these interpersonal and structural power dynamics, differences between siblings can become exaggerated through the ascription of mutually exclusive, oppositional labels. We saw this in the construction of Anna as the 'loud', 'clever' one, leaving Francesca being 'not so smart'. Young people commonly referred to a naughty or good 'one' when talking about themselves and their siblings. As 12-year-old Nick states of his older sisters, 'Er Sara outside ... she was like the good one. Rebecca, she's the really naughty one. Rebecca got excluded [from school] about, I think it's 27 times.' It is significant that there is rarely a good two or three when it comes to describing sibling identities in common parlance. Take the following discussion in which Sadia (a 14-year-old British Pakistani girl, interviewed at Highfields school, who has two older brothers and four older sisters and who currently lives with her father and

two of her sisters) is describing herself in relation to the two sisters
she lives with:

> Sadia: [discussing the older of the two sisters] She's really argumentative.
> She wouldn't like give in. Erm, she likes going out and just being by
> herself most of the time.
>
> ...
>
> Interviewer: What about your other sister?
>
> Sadia: Erm, she compromises us both. She does like, she mainly does
> all the work at home. She helps me out as well with my dad and
> everything else. She's like the good one.
>
> ...
>
> Interviewer: So if she's the good one, what one are you would you
> say?
>
> Sadia: Erm, I think I'm the naughty one...

The way Sadia describes one sister as 'compromising' the other less
helpful and well-behaved sisters is illuminating in that it suggests
an understanding that, when taken together, the characteristics of
the three sisters form a well-balanced whole. Sadia is the 'naughty
one' *because* her sisters are not, and this identity is of course
also constructed within the complex gendered dynamics of these
relationships.

Thus it seems that in narrating themselves and their sibling(s) in
terms of being the naughty, quiet, good or clever 'one', young people
are constructing their own characteristics in relation to the sibship
as a whole. These ways that young people narrated their own and
their siblings' identities point to the centrality of sameness and
difference in sibling relations, with individuality constructed in
relation to the sibling group. As outlined in Chapter 1, Edwards
and colleagues made a similar point in their study of sibling relationships in middle childhood, identifying the casual, everyday ways in
which siblings compare themselves and are compared to each other
in families, with 'sameness and difference' described as 'two of the
key intersubjective notions that children and young people use when
describing and reflecting upon their own sense of self' (2006: 38).
The role of observing and 'knowing' the character of one's siblings
in shaping the self echoes Sasha Roseneil and Kaisa Ketokivi's (2006)

emphasis on individual creativity and reflexivity in the formation of the self, whereby people reflect on their own actions in relation to others, thus making sense of their own behaviour and achievements as well as attributes and character in relation to their siblings. Thus these practices of relational reflexivity can be understood as contributing to processes of comparing between siblings in conjunction with the labelling of siblings by others.

As well as constructing these comparisons around aspects of character, it was also common for young participants to narrate themselves in terms of how they are similar or different in appearance to their siblings. For example, discussing her brother, Lois stated that 'everyone says I look like him in the face, I've got his nose, I've got his eyes, I've got his lips' and Poppy summed up the differences between her and her sister by relating their appearance to that of their parents: 'I look like my dad, and my sister looks like my mum when my mum was little.' In the following example, 11-year-old Georgia (who is white British, was interviewed at the rural youth club and has one half-brother and one half-sister) cites physical attractiveness and build as a way of differentiating herself from her half-sister and of explaining their differing levels of social success at school:

> Georgia: Erm, my brother's, like, sort of the good looking boy out of everybody else sort of thing, except he looks like my dad ... Actually, he looks like me. My sister ... she's quite short and, erm, she's like pretty big, so she's a bit different to me cos of that sort of thing ... so she's obviously a bit different to me at school.

Here Georgia is conceptualising the appearance of her siblings in relation to the sibship as a whole in a similar way to Sadia's description of being the 'naughty one' earlier. The complexities of family resemblances and theories about who takes after who and how and why things get passed on in families are clearly woven into Georgia's narrative of the relational construction of her siblings' selves at school. She provides these categorisations with an explanatory history and indicates the entwining of physicality and character in the construction of sibling similarities and differences. In Chapter 4 I explore how people apply what Jeanette Edwards (2000) terms 'kinship expertise' in constructing rules about how siblings might turn out in life, and in Chapter 3 I consider resemblances as part of the fabric of relationships, pertaining to feelings of connectedness and relatedness. Here, I focus on the comparability of siblings and the role of resemblance and difference with siblings in shaping people's sense of who they are.

In her exploration of the role of race and perceptions of differences in racial, ethnic and religious identification among mixed-race siblings, Miri Song (2010) points to the ways siblings in her study used various markers of difference when constructing their identities in relation to their siblings, including the use of ethnic and racial terms. Some siblings were seen as more or less 'white', 'black' or 'Chinese' compared to their brothers or sisters, based on differences in friends, religious observance, taste in music and food as well as physical appearance. Thus, the emphasis on similarities and differences in sibling relationships influenced the racial and ethnic identification of siblings.

Of course, people compare themselves to a range of others, including friends, but there is something unique about siblings here. As outlined in the introduction, the comparability of siblings is enhanced by the fact that they often share the same upbringing and genes, inviting people to speculate about how differences might arise, and what similarities and differences between full, step- and half-siblings can tell us about questions of nature and nurture, which, as Jennifer Mason (2008) explains, are endlessly fascinating. As Janet Carsten identifies, full siblings are unique in that they 'start the same' before becoming 'different and separate' (1997: 106). Thus, comparability, inherently part of siblingship since birth, is part and parcel of observing how a child is progressing towards adulthood and beyond, and by comparing siblings it is possible to unlock some of the mysteries of how we turn out the way we do.

This comparability is something that people can be highly reflexive about, as it becomes part of their story of who they are and why, and theories are developed around this. Mass observer F1566, for example, wrote about her theory that the years between birth and age two are crucial, and that this period of early life explains why, despite differences between them, her and her sibling have not, as she put it, 'broken down and [have instead] enjoyed relatively good mental health'. Another describes the differences between herself and her sister, putting these down simply 'to genes', a shorthand for the 'ineffable mysteries of kinship' identified by Mason (2018) and discussed in more detail in Chapter 4.

All the focus groups with young people included discussions about *how* this comparing can occur. Take the following focus group discussion with young people aged 14–15 years old at St Stephen's school, where participants debated the pattern of these comparing practices:

> Interviewer: What are the advantages and disadvantages of being the youngest do you think?
>
> Participant 1: [inaudible] pressure to be like your older brother or sister.
>
> Interviewer: Right. So this pressure ... is that worse if you've got an older brother or sister?
>
> Participant 1: Probably cos it's like you should be more like them.
>
> Participant 2: Yeah but not always cos the oldest is always compared to the parents.
>
> Interviewer: Do you think?
>
> Participant 2: Yeah, because there's no-one else.
>
> ...
>
> Participant 1: Yeah, but the younger child can be compared with the older one. So it's a lot like closer.
>
> ...
>
> Participant 3: Sometimes the younger children are compared to the adults though aren't they?
>
> Participant 4: To the parents.

This discussion conveys the idea that comparing between siblings is an inevitability which affects young people's experiences of growing up as a sibling. The young people in this focus group are not only aware of this comparing but look for patterns or rules in making sense of who is compared to whom within families. These patterns relate to family structures (birth order and generational positioning), even if there is little agreement about what these patterns are. Important here is the idea that these patterns and practices of comparing result in feelings of being under pressure, affecting the experience of birth order and implicating self/identity.

The construction of identity in relation to siblings presents something of a conundrum when considered alongside what Edwards and colleagues describe as the Western ideal of personhood, which rests on 'individuality, autonomy and independence' (2006: 39). Anna after all could only be 'naturally' outgoing with possession of a 'backbone' *because* Francesca was constructed as not having these elements, so her narrative of a naturally strong and individual self was in fact relationally constructed. In his account of the 'culture of authenticity', Charles Taylor writes:

> There is a certain way of being human that is *my* way. I am called upon to live my life in this way, and not in imitation of anyone else's. But this gives a new importance to being true to myself. If I am not, I miss the point of my life, I miss what being human is for *me*. (1991: 28–9)

For Taylor, the culture of authenticity is given 'moral force' (1991: 29) by the idea that it is crucial to be in contact with yourself, to stay true to your own 'inner nature' (1991: 28) and originality (which the individual must discover and articulate for themselves). Taylor identifies a paradox here as, although it might appear that identity is entirely the project of the individual, it is of course relationally constructed:

> We are expected to develop our own opinions, outlook, stances to things, to a considerable degree through solitary reflection. But this is not how things work with important issues, such as the definition of our identity. We define this always in dialogue with, sometimes in struggle against, the identities our significant others want to recognise in us. And even when we outgrow some of the latter – our parents, for instance – and they disappear from our lives, the conversation with them continues within us as long as we live. (1991: 33)

For siblings, whose comparability can be heightened by generational and genetic proximity as well as shared upbringing, this paradox can be profoundly felt, and Edwards and colleagues turn to psychoanalysis in the work of Juliet Mitchell, Prophecy Coles and Sigmund Freud to explore the internal and emotional struggles brought about by similarity and difference, pointing to how children in their study – who emphasised the differences between themselves and their siblings – experienced more conflictual and competitive relationships. Edwards and colleagues also explore the cultural nuances of this, demonstrating through the example of a sibship of five South Asian sisters how gender, culture and, in this case, the sisters' Muslim religion intersected with their role as siblings in their emphasis on their commonalities and sense of shared reputation to create a feeling of interdependence, with siblings in this case 'literally becoming part of the self' (Edwards et al., 2006: 46). In other cultural contexts, there may be no paradox. In Janet Carsten's ethnography of a Malaysian fishing village, for example, concepts of similarity and difference in sibling relationships are not problematic and instead represent kinship. Carsten writes: 'Siblingsip is both about resemblance and identity and about differences. Simultaneously individuals and multiple, it is the process by which things start the same, multiple entities in one body, but become different and separate, bodies within bodies' (1997: 106). So in this context there is no battle between the unique self and being part of a sibship. Siblings are simultaneously individual and mutual and this is because they represent birth, kinship and what it means to be related.

Nikolas Rose also points to the culture of the 'true', 'authentic', 'inner' self in Western society, pointing out its production through Western culture by evidencing its discursive nature. Rose traces how this version of the self is produced and perpetuated by the rise of the psy-sciences such as psychology, psychoanalysis and psychotherapy, with individuals coming 'to interrogate and narrate themselves in terms of a psychological "inner life" that holds the secrets of their identity' (1996: 22). As with Taylor, for Rose there is also a moral or ethical element to this:

> Within contemporary political rationalities and technologies of government, the freedom of subjects is more than merely an ideology. Subjects are *obliged* to be 'free', to construe their existence as the outcome of choices that they make among a plurality of alternatives. (Rose, 1996: 79)

Thus, the comparability of siblings and the ways they are narrated and understood in terms of their seriality threatens their obligation to be a 'free' individual, able to follow their own path. This helps us to understand why siblings often try to resist being compared by teachers and parents. We also see people narrating their own sense of identity in terms of a 'true', fixed, inner self – Anna's 'backbone' being a good example.

Of course, in order to make these points about comparability, generalisations have been made, and Edwards and colleagues' (2006) example indicates the cultural particularities of comparing among South Asian siblings. Song's (2010) study of mixed-race siblings also revealed huge differences between families, with some seeing differences in ethnic and racial identification between siblings as highly significant while others did not place importance on such differences or did not register differences at all. There are also classed elements to the contexts in which resemblances between siblings are resisted and welcomed, and I return to this point in more detail towards the end of this chapter in relation to the role of the local community in the construction of sibling identity.

In discussing what it is about siblings that makes them invite comparison, I have mentioned generational as well as genetic proximity – with siblings who are brought up in the same house by the same parents and with shared genetic heritage often assumed to be more likely to turn out to be similar. What is interesting is that this assumption is not limited to full siblings. Many young people who I spoke to, as well as the mass observers, talked about their half-siblings in terms of similarity as well as difference. Research by Carsten (2000) on reunions between 'long-lost' siblings has also indicated how siblings search for similarities despite the absence of a shared upbringing. The fascination with long-lost siblings mentioned in the introduction resonates with the mystery and wonder of kinship identified by Mason (2008; 2018).

Most of the examples cited thus far have indicated the role of others in the construction of sibling relational identities, from the ways participants appeared to be reproducing well-rehearsed narratives when reciting the similarities and differences between themselves and their siblings to the specific references to teachers' and parents' habit of comparing siblings. The comparisons of others were generally readily adopted by young people and often seemed to form a taken-for-granted aspect of their kinship knowledge. This is epitomised in Lois's use of the phrase 'everyone says' when discussing her physical likeness to her brother in the quotation cited earlier, and in both Anna's and Francesca's narratives, which are imbued with the voices of their father, mother and grandmother as well as one another in how they make sense of and narrate their differences.

The role of others in the construction of similarity and difference between siblings indicates the embedding of siblingship within wider networks of relationships. But how are these narratives of similarity and difference perpetuated and how do they relate to wider familial power dynamics? In the following section I turn to work that explores the social significance of stories in order to start to theorise *how* these relational sibling identities can be constructed.

The role of stories in the construction of sibling identities

Family stories are the gist of social description, the raw material for both history and social change; but we need to listen to them more attentively than that. They are also the symbolic coinage of exchange between the generations, of family transmission. They may haunt, or inspire, or be taken as commonplace. But the way in which they are told, the stories and images which are chosen and put together, and the matters on which silence is kept provide part of the mental map of family members … Family myths, models, and denials, transmitted within a family system provide for most people part of the context in which their crucial life choices must be made, propelling them into their own individual life paths. (Thompson, 1993: 36)

For Paul Thompson, family stories are the fabric of the social world, forming the context for individual life choices and decisions. Others have similarly examined the link between stories and self; Stephanie Lawler (2008) and James A. Holstein and Jaber F. Gubrium (2000), for example, point to the effect of stories on individuals, with both arguing that identity is created through narrative. The self, according to Holstein and Gubrium, 'is not only something we are, but an object we *actively* construct and live by' (2000: 10, original emphasis) through everyday 'narrative practice' (2000: 104). Important to understandings of stories are the ways in which they are produced collectively, and as such are subject to the politics and power dynamics of the interpersonal relationships within which they are created. Barbara Misztal, for example, discusses how memory is constructed communally through the telling of stories in 'mnemonic communities'; 'groups that socialize us to what should be remembered and what should be forgotten' (2003: 15). Song (2010) also highlights the role of family scripts in the construction of mixed-race siblings' ethnic identities. Therefore, stories are part of how relationality comes to affect individuals and the ways they act upon themselves.

The construction, telling and retelling of stories within families can be a mechanism through which siblings' relational identities can be produced and reproduced. A sense of this was gained in the ways interview and focus group participants reproduced rehearsed narratives when describing their similarities to and differences from their sibling(s). Anna's and Francesca's accounts of their own resemblances and differences can also be read as stories; Francesca (re)producing a narrative of resemblance to her father and, consequently, of difference from her sister and mother, and Anna appearing to create herself a narrative of similarities with her 6-year-old half-sister. These resemblance stories work to produce and reproduce kinship, and I return to this issue in the following chapter. Here the focus remains on the work of these narratives in (re)producing the self.

Young people have considerable agency in the creation and telling of these narratives and do not simply reproduce the stories of others. Indeed, Anna's narrative of similarity with her half-sister seems to be within her control, and she puts it to work in the presentation of herself as 'loud' and outgoing. Mass observer C3210 is a 32-year-old woman with an identical twin. She focuses on how, despite being identical twins, she and her sister suit different hairstyles and colours and now look very different. She is also extremely critical of those who treated her and her sister as 'one person' when they were younger due to their similarities, describing it as 'very rude' and criticising parents who dress their twins in matching clothes. In this example, it seems that the ability to successfully resist these narratives of similarity, compounded and reinforced by the evidential nature of physical resemblances between twins, exists only in adulthood, where the observer and her twin sister were able to tell stories about difference as well as cultivating different appearances. Such stories of resistance occurred less commonly than those where participants seemed to be reproducing narratives provided by others (usually parents). Take the following example, in which 12-year-old Britney is discussing her cousin Joseph (who she describes as being 'like' a brother). Although Britney is critical of her mother and uncle for comparing her to Joseph and attempts to reclaim the narrative by pointing to her own unique talents, she ultimately accepts their depiction of Joseph as more intelligent:

> Britney: Like I get it a lot cos he's really smart and I'm not. I'm like more of the chatty person. He's the one that concentrates and gets down, buckles down. And like my mum and uncle Nigel and everyone's like, 'Why can't you be more like Joseph?' and it drives me insane. That really does get on my nerves cos I've had it said to me so much I'm like, 'Well I'm trying: Don't you, don't you listen to what I'm saying?' I'm good at art. He's not. We're different.

Here we see the lateral nature of Britney and Joseph's cousin relationship inviting comparison in the same ways as we have seen with siblings throughout this chapter.

The ways in which stories are constructed within the dynamics and politics of existing relationships came across clearly in those interviews conducted with a parent present. In these interviews young people appeared to have less power to control the story that was told, and were often interrupted or corrected by their parent when they strayed from existing family scripts. The attempts of Aiden, aged 12, to describe his siblings are a good example of this. Not only do we see him incorporating his mother's descriptions into his narrative but we see her dictating the sorts of characteristics discussed:

> Aiden: Er, Claire, she's, like, really into drawing. David, he's.
>
> Mother: No, what's her personality, like though?
>
> Aiden: Like, happy, as well as me.
>
> Mother: She's very sensitive, isn't she?
>
> Aiden: Like, sensitive as well. David is, like grumpy … Chelsea, erm, she's more like, getting into boyfriends, and stuff like that. And Amy.
>
> Mother: You don't really know, do you? She hasn't lived at home for a while, has she?
>
> Aiden: I don't really know.

Having a parent present during interviews created what Gubrium and Holstein (2009) would term a different 'narrative environment', and the stories generated by these interviews reflect this difference. I now examine a particular interview in which parent–child interactions occurred throughout to explore the dynamics of power in these 'narrative environments' in more detail. By analysing one interview as a whole it is possible to illuminate *how* stories of sibling relational identity can be constructed within complex webs of relationships.

Politics and power in the communal construction of family stories: the case of Mason and his half-brother

The politics and power dynamics at the heart of stories about siblings' relational identities were particularly observable in an interview at home with Mason (aged 13 and recruited through Romsbridge school), where his mother, who sat in on most of the interview, interjected during a discussion about similarities and differences between Mason and his half-brother. Mason's mother and father are divorced (Mason, who is white British and from a working-class background, lives with his mother but sees his father regularly) and he has a half-brother, Zack, from another relationship of his father's. Zack is one year older than Mason and attends the same school, although they have never lived together. The discussion between Mason, his mother and the interviewer offers insights into how and why a narrative about the differences between Mason and his half-brother might have been collectively constructed:

> Mother: And they're [Mason and Zack] completely opposite. You both went to the same school and the teachers can't believe you're brothers.
>
> ...
>
> Mason: [We're] really, like, different and they [school teachers] expect me to be like my brother. Like, good at art and not that good at maths and English. But it's the opposite for me; I'm not that good at art, but I'm good at maths and English.
>
> ...
>
> Mother: He is [good at art]. But he thinks he's not better than Zack.
>
> Mason: I'm not, I'm not that good though.
>
> Mother: No, but you've done very good.
>
> ...

Mother: That's, sorry, that's the only feedback I got when I went to his parents' evening in March, no one could believe that he ... they can't believe that Zack is his brother. That's all we got.

Interviewer: [to Mason]: What do you think of that?

Mother: And the mannerisms. And I didn't understand at first, and I said, cos he's [Zack] lovely with me, but I'm very strict, well not strict, but I don't have children talking back. So he, when he comes, when he's been here he's lovely with me, but outside that door, he's completely...

In this example, a multitude of voices (Mason's, his mother's and the children's teachers) contribute to the narrative of Mason and Zack as very different. Mason and his mother are in agreement that the brothers are different, but whereas Mason concentrates on academic differences, his mother focuses on differences in character, mannerisms and, ultimately, upbringing. It is also clear that it is the mother's voice that dominates, and my attempts as the interviewer to provide Mason with the opportunity to contribute his own take on his differences from Zack largely failed, with his mother jumping in to respond to questions on his behalf. The relative powerlessness of the young people in the story is notable and the dominant role of Mason's mother in the interaction provides a 'live' example of her power in shaping the story that is told. It is also notable that Mason's mother draws on the comparing practices of teachers to corroborate her own account, pointing to the powerful role that teachers play, almost as 'experts' on sibling comparison, which serve as a narrative device, strengthening her version of the story.

It is likely that Mason's mother has strong motivations for wanting to construct the two brothers as different. First, she seems eager to boost Mason's confidence and ensure he sees himself as equal, if not superior, in intelligence and academic success to Zack (she rejects the narrative of the brothers having different skills and insists that Mason is also good at art). Secondly, she is divorced from Mason's father, and by constructing his son, Zack, as badly behaved and Mason as different, she is able to draw attention to differences she perceives between her own and her ex-partner's parenting skills. As such, a narrative is produced constructing the brothers as opposites and creating relational memories about what the boys were like at school and when growing up more generally.

This example indicates *how* stories about sibling identities can come to be formed within families and the role of power and generation in this, illustrating how stories are embedded within existing relationships and relational histories. Like Anna and Francesca, Mason and Zack's identities are sedimented into the history of Mason's parents' relationship with one another. Thus, sibling identities can be constructed not only in relation to other siblings in the family but also in relation to complex webs of relationships with and between others formed over time. In other words, young people's lives are fundamentally relational, embedded and linked (Bengtson et al., 2002).

The carrying over of identity and reputation

In explaining how sibling identity can be constructed in relation to the sibship as a whole, I touched upon the role of school and teachers in comparing siblings. Here I focus on how having a sibling can affect how one is seen by others, as the reputation, characteristics and attributes of one's siblings can 'rub off', attaching themselves to one's own identity, limiting the possibilities for performing the self and affecting how one is perceived by others. This rubbing off was felt particularly strongly at school but could also impact upon siblings' identities in their local communities. Young people spoke in interviews and focus groups about how having a sibling who was known to teachers and peers at school meant that their sibling's reputation could rub off on them, affecting how they themselves were perceived, both in terms of being recognised as a particular person's sibling as well as being seen to somehow embody aspects of a sibling's reputation. This 'known-ness' is enhanced when siblings look alike, the physical resemblance encouraging others to make a connection between them and to assume other similarities, as well as making the sibling connection public and readily observable. Jennifer Mason identifies a public fascination with resemblances, which are 'in some ways deeply personal but are also publicly perceived, constructed, commented on and speculated about' (2008: 30). As physical resemblances are *'highly charged with kinship'* (Mason, 2008: 31, original emphasis), their evidential nature means that what Carsten (2004) would term the 'substance' of kinship (blood, genes, biogenetic substances) is implicated in young people's reputation and identity at school when they are seen to resemble their sibling(s). Diana Marre and Joan Bestard (2009) describe this as the recognition of the 'family body', tying together the social identities of family members. Thus, when siblings are seen by peers and teachers to look alike, they are often assumed to be alike in other ways.

This can happen with peers, when having a sibling who is known by others due to their popularity can help their younger siblings to be socially successful at school, and it was possible for young people to garner more respect from their peers due to the reputation of their sibling. Take the following comment made by Tom (age 16, estate youth club) about why he thinks people might feel positive about a physical resemblance with an older brother:

> Cos you get known for it … Like, if your brother's known … Because, like, if your big brother's, like, known, and then all like, everyone who hangs about with your brother like knows you because of your big brother.

Molly and Lois, aged 14 and also interviewed at the estate youth club, expressed similar views about the benefits to one's reputation of sharing a physical resemblance with a sibling, which they describe as 'nice', this time based on Lois's experiences with her older brother, who is well known at school and in the local neighbourhood:

> Interviewer: Why do you think it's nice to, kind of, look like people? Have you got any theory?
>
> Molly: Cos then people say, 'Oh I saw you before' and then they look at you, they can go, 'Oh you're so and so's little sister' so they know you then…
>
> Lois: That's what I mean, because, like, if they respect your brother they're going to respect you if you look a bit like him aren't you, as well?

Significantly the idea of 'known-ness' came across most strongly in the accounts of young people interviewed at the estate youth club where participants spoke of the rubbing off of this stigmatised place on their reputations at school, and where being known within the community of the estate was important in this context of deprivation and stigmatisation. The centrality of older brothers in these discussions of known-ness is reminiscent of gendered norms around 'protection' and indicates the complexities of gender in the rubbing off of reputation which occurred between mixed and same-sex siblings. Edwards and colleagues point to the importance of everyday interactions in the local community as a space where identities are constructed:

> it was striking how much of the to and fro of their [the siblings in their research] interactions went on beyond the living room and the bedroom, to include the street, the stairways and walkways of flats, the homes of neighbours, friends and wider family, parks, shopping centres and out of school classes. (2006: 102)

Edwards and colleagues note how siblings were often implicated in the 'moral reputations' of children in their locality. Their participants often spoke about being 'shown up' (2006: 107) by their sibling when out, and the authors note how gender intersected with ethnicity and culture in the ways their participants experienced siblingship in place. As discussed earlier in this chapter, others have also highlighted the significance of family reputation in South Asian communities, with emphasis on the gendered nature of how the identity of one family member can impact on the family as a whole (Shaw, 2000; Bhopal, 1997). In her analysis of the role of racial and ethnic identification in the relational construction of identity among mixed-race siblings, Song points to how siblings' 'ethnic and racial identifications, as well as their family reputations more generally, are formed in relation to one another over the course of family life' (2010: 267).

Teachers were also implicated in the 'rubbing off' of reputation between siblings. Many young people talked in interviews of being likened to a brother or sister (including half- and step-siblings) by teachers at school, or having witnessed this happening to others, and it was discussed as a common practice in all focus groups. This likening was seen as impacting upon the way teachers viewed young people's behaviour, intelligence and attitude to school. Many participants attested to concerns that teachers might think less of them if their sibling's reputation at school is not positive and they are not seen as intelligent or well behaved. As Craig (age 14, white British, estate youth club) commented, he is pleased that he does not attend the same school as his older brothers and sisters because 'if I went their school, they'd all expect me to be like them. I'd have to, like, well, live *down* to their reputation cos mine's better than theirs.' Others who had siblings who had 'good' reputations saw comparisons and assumptions of similarity as beneficial to their standing with teachers. Sadia (age 14, Pakistani British, Highfields), for example, described how she likes it when teachers remember her older sisters because they are likely to say things like 'they were wonderful and you're really alike'. As Molly (age 14, estate youth club) summarises, 'it depends if they've been naughty or good in school don't it really?'

This transference through the rubbing off of an older sibling's reputation indicates a proximity between siblings that implicates their identity and that is an unintended consequence of the sibling relationship, and one over which young people have little control. There are similarities here with the ways older siblings can be a benchmark in the comparing of siblings who are obviously related due to looking alike or sharing a surname. This means that siblings often experience a particularly 'sticky' sort of relational proximity that can carry over into the context of school or community and cannot be 'shaken off', bringing a young person's sibling into their everyday experiences even if they are not physically together. This public rubbing off of characteristics from one sibling to another is likely to impact upon their experiences of school and community in terms of their friendships and relationships with teachers, as well as implicating their perceptions of their own talents and capabilities more generally.

Conclusion

This chapter has identified how the comparative nature of sibling relationships can render them fundamental to the formation of self/ identity. We often make sense of who we are in relation to how we are similar to or different from our siblings, and others often understand us in this way too. This can cause something of a paradox when these aspects of being one in a series of siblings are considered alongside the Western ideal of the autonomous individual self. This chapter has also indicated how these practices of comparing take place within the power dynamics of interpersonal relationships. Furthermore, the sometimes evidential nature of relatedness with siblings, which often manifests in physical resemblances, can mean the rubbing off of characteristics and attributes between siblings in different settings, implicating reputation, identity and self.

By thinking with siblings about the meanings and constructions of sociological concepts of self and identity, this chapter has indicated the importance of looking horizontally for sources of influence beyond that of parents. In emphasising the significance of lateral kin to sociological understandings of the self I do not wish to suggest that vertical relationships are without importance. Indeed, this chapter has demonstrated that parents in particular can play a key role in the construction of the family stories and memories that create relational identities. It is also notable that parents seem to possess more power than children here (although this is not to deny that children are agentic social actors in these processes). However, the particular comparability of siblings means that they comprise a *particularly* significant 'other', influencing identification and self-classification in ways that the existing sociological preoccupation with intergenerational influence overlooks. I suggest that, in thinking through how processes of socialisation occur, sociologists must widen their gaze to look beyond the prominence of parents in accounts such as those proposed by Mead (1934) and Bourdieu (1990) and ensure that lateral relationships are accounted for.

Furthermore, this chapter has demonstrated that to fully appreciate the role of lateral kin in the formation of the self is not a question of simply looking horizontally as well as vertically, although this is important, and the sociological blind spot in this direction of transmission means we might have to make a conscious effort to look both ways in our thinking. Rather, it is about conceptualising the self as formed through webs of connection over time, as emphasised by sociologists such as Smart (2007) and Mason (2004) in their discussion of embeddedness and relationality. Focusing on siblings can therefore push our sociological thinking about the formation of the self in new directions, forcing us to consider the ways that proximities in age, context (such as school, home or neighbourhood), relationality as well as genetics combine in the formation of the self.

Indeed, using siblings as a tool to think with has facilitated a different way of looking at the contextual performance of identity in different settings. In exploring how the 'rubbing off' and 'carrying over' of identity between contexts is implicated by a sense of genetic relatedness that can be 'read' from physical resemblances, looking at siblings invites sociologists to incorporate embodied, genetic and sensory elements into our analyses of the social self. This is partially why siblingship can be such a fruitful topic of sociological inquiry, helping us to understand relational identity construction, not just in terms of social interactionism but also in ways that reach beyond the social to include genetic relatedness, physical resemblance and the sharing of blood. These elements will be further explored in the next chapter which contemplates what it means to be a sibling.

Chapter 3

Relationality

Questions of what it means to be related pervade all sibling relationships in some way. Whether close or distant, linked by shared genes, upbringing or neither, siblings bring to the fore some of the conundrums of relationality. How are sibling relationships lived and experienced? How does the meaning and doing of siblingship change in different contexts and situations? What does it mean for siblings to be described as 'close' and how is the experience of being and having siblings embodied and sensorial? In addressing these questions, this chapter contemplates the meanings of relatedness between siblings, reflecting on how people make sense of who is and isn't a sibling, considering the uncanny role of resemblance between siblings and exploring the role of ethereal or otherworldly connections.

In exploring the meaning of sibling relationships it is important to recognise that they are imbued with emotion. In the introduction I pointed to some of the fictional depictions of sibling relationships which often emphasise emotions such as love and support (the sisters in the popular 2013 Disney film *Frozen*) and jealousy (the various reworkings of the central themes of the biblical story of Cain and Abel). Media depictions of famous siblings often perpetuate a preoccupation with rifts and disagreements, and we see this in the British media obsession with a so-called rift between princes William and Harry which has resulted in countless media articles, television 'documentaries' and books (Lacey, 2020).

Siblingship is illuminating for sociologists interested in exploring the meaning and experience of relatedness because, in addition to the intensity of emotions at the centre of siblingship in the public imagination, sibling relationships are particularly complicated, changeable and contradictory. Sibling relationships are unique in the general societal agreement, at least in the West, that conflict, even physical violence, can be a day-to-day part of a 'normal' sibling relationship. Every parenting book worth its salt includes a section on dealing with sibling conflict, with a whole subsection of parenting books devoted to this issue (see, for example, Jan Parker and Jan Stimpson's 2002 book *Raising Happy Brothers and Sisters* and Adele Faber and Elaine Mazlish's 1998 book *Siblings Without Rivalry*) and countless threads on the online forum Mumsnet with titles such as 'Sibling rivalry' and 'What to do about sibling bullying' attracting hundreds of comments. This conflict is often understood as an inevitable part of the everyday fabric of sibling relationships. Alongside this seemingly inevitable conflict, sibling relationships can also be characterised by care, which similarly takes different forms, from a kind of background, ever-present 'being there' (Brownlie, 2014), to a more active source of support in certain contexts such as school holiday clubs. These complexities reveal the importance of developing a contextual understanding of seemingly contradictory sibling relationships. Indeed, sibling relationships can help us to question taken-for-granted ideas about what 'closeness' means, challenging the idea that the low-level background support that characterises being there is somehow *less than* the seemingly deeper connections of disclosing intimacies that characterise Liz Spencer and Ray Pahl's (2006) highly complex 'soulmate' friend or Anthony Giddens's (1992) pure relationship, and widening definitions of a close relationship to incorporate conflict and ambivalence.

The meaning and experience of relatedness between siblings can be both fixed and fluid. For example, step- and half-siblings – along with close family friends and cousins – can feel like 'real' siblings or not, depending on a range of factors, including a sense of shared childhood, revealing something about the meaning of relatedness. In this chapter I explore these complexities of the meanings and experiences of sibling relationships, from the ups and downs of everyday life as a sibling to how siblings care for one another, and the ways siblingship is done and enacted in different contexts. The chapter also explores the significance of material and embodied aspects of the sibling relationship as well as the meaning of resemblances and affinities that can feel magical or otherworldly.

The ups and downs of sibling relationships

Caring and 'being there' for one another

Feelings of annoyance and irritation are a common feature of many sibling relationships in childhood. Ros Edwards and colleagues (2006) found many descriptions of siblings by children in their study such as 'annoying', 'she bugs me', 'he winds me up'. The authors suggest that these constructions of sibling behaviours as annoying were often linked to age as well as social class. Hayley Davies also considers the role of sensory, embodied and inter-physical experiences in children's reflections of their interactions with their siblings as 'annoying' (2015: 71; see also Punch, 2005). When asked to describe their siblings in interviews or focus groups in my study, 'annoying' was by far the most common response that young people gave. Mass observers also often commented on the ways in which, though still capable of proving highly irritating in adulthood, their annoyance with their siblings peaked in childhood. Annoying siblings are also something of a cultural trope with which people can interact when narrating their own sibling relationships; annoying siblings are often depicted in children's television and literature, including the popular UK children's book and cartoon series *Horrid Henry*, in which one of the protagonists, Henry's little brother 'Perfect Peter', epitomises the irritation of having a younger sibling who always seems to win favour from parents and teachers. Annoying older siblings who exist *in loco parentis* to spoil the fun are also a common feature of fictional depictions of teenage life, such as the up-tight older sibling in the 1986 teen film *Ferris Bueller's Day Off* who acts as a foil to Ferris's fun-loving free spirit for much of the plot, and the Weasleys' humourless, school prefect older brother Percy, in J. K. Rowling's *Harry Potter* series. The prevalence of these cultural tropes about children's annoying siblings means that feelings of irritation are often an accepted and taken-for-granted facet of sibling relationships.

Fictional depictions of annoying sibling relationships often also include glimpses of solidarity or closeness, and this ability to be at once annoyed by a sibling while also experiencing a relationship that has feelings of closeness and care is a common feature of siblingship. Eva Gulløv, Charlotte Palludan and Ida Wentzel Winther (2015) point to this in their account of the complex and shifting nature of everyday sibling relationships, describing the 'frictions' that characterise the co-presence of both tension and commitment in sibling relationships. The concept of friction allowed them 'to investigate the social micro-climate of siblings and make sense of the ambiguous emotional practices the informants speak of in relation to their sibling relationships' (2015: 511). The authors differentiate between 'regular', 'intense' and 'downplayed' frictions that were raised by young participants in their study of sibling relationships and divorce, but emphasise the ways that these exist alongside commitment, tenderness, loyalty and care, so that '[e]ven when troublesome incidents are retold, in most cases we register a tone of close connection and inseparability' (2015: 516).

Indeed, many young people I spoke to in interviews and focus groups described their sibling relationships as imbued with both care and annoyance, with care often experienced as a kind of background 'being there' that is not reliant on a friendly relationship and can coexist with annoyance and irritation. This comes across clearly in the following example in which Courtney, a 15-year-old girl who has five siblings, in an interview with her friend Emily, is talking about how, despite being annoying, her little brothers look after her:

Courtney: They look after you, like, my little brothers do look after me.

...

Interviewer: Oh, okay, so it's not necessarily, they don't have to be older to look after you...

Emily: They can be younger.

Courtney: And, well, the thing I hate about them is they're annoying. They're really, really annoying.

The kind of care exchanged between siblings often takes the form of small, seemingly inconsequential offerings that add up to a feeling of being there. In her exploration of the 'ordinary relationships in which our emotional lives are embedded' (2014: 2), Julie Brownlie unpacks what it means when we say that someone is 'there' for us. Being there in everyday life, according to Brownlie, can be a taken-for-granted, mundane set of practices that constitute emotional support and signify a meaningful relationship. Brownlie's being there is not centred on talk, and instead the 'there-ness' involves a sense of 'reachability' in principle, even if it is not used in practice, alongside a range of mundane – but no less significant – care-giving practices such as financial help or help with moving house, as well as the idea that shared experiences can give a sense of privileged knowledge or a feeling that the person is somehow 'on our side' (2014: 135). Brownlie also points to being there as a sense of *'being alongside'* (2014: 137, original emphasis) – an idea of 'there-ness' which does not necessarily involve an active doing or saying and which, as Brownlie points out, can cover 'low-level or background emotions such as feelings of security, implicit trust and acceptance' (2014: 148). In the film that accompanies their 2015 monograph *(Ex)changeable Siblingship: Experienced and Practiced by Children and Young People in Denmark*, Ida Wentzer Winther, Charlotte Palluden, Eva Gulløv and Mads Middelboe Rehder show the children of divorced and separated parents travelling between their parents' homes. It is clear that the children and young people in the film are reassured by the presence of their sibling(s) on these journeys. As one of the young people (19-year-old Louise) explains, despite her conflict with her sister, 'You always feel that you have someone close to you and someone who can help you – you never feel, you know, all alone' (2015b: 85).

This sense of closeness and 'there-ness' is present in the following focus group discussion in which young people are reflecting on the various ways that their siblings are there for them in the present, as well as their expectations surrounding this for the future:

Participant 1: Erm, say like if when, after you've grown up and your like parents passed away, it's like you won't be alone and stuff you'll still have your family.

Participant 2: If you're like stuck on something then you, your like brothers and sisters could actually help you ... Like with your homework.

Participant 3: Say if you're, erm, being bullied, like say in Year 8, or Year 7, and they're say a Year 10, they'll be scared of them. So you can help each other out with like bullying and stuff.

Participant 4: Erm, like if they've got more money they could lend you some.

Participant 5: If you've got no like, er, friends who are like walking your way home you could walk home with them. [ages 11–12, St Stephen's]

Here we see many examples of care passing between siblings that echo those identified by Brownlie as part of being there, from day-to-day help with homework to support that can be drawn upon in response to bullying, from a sense of permanence in the prediction of future need to the quite literal 'walking alongside' when there is no one else. Brownlie's work is helpful in making sense of the ways siblings can be a background presence, even where relationships are not characterised by emotional 'closeness' in the more commonly thought of talk-based ways. In this example, siblings were there to provide practical help when necessary (help with homework and borrowing money) as well as a sense of 'being alongside', now and in the future, which manifested in a general feeling of not being alone at key points in the life course, such as on the death of one's parents or in more everyday mundane activities such as walking home from school. The idea that siblings were 'reachable' (Brownlie, 2014), there to draw support from if necessary, was also expressed by mass observers, with a number writing that their sibling would be there as a source of support if needed. This knowledge that a sibling would be there did not have to exist as part of a relationship that had always been defined as loving and caring – one mass observer (C36991), who felt that her sister would 'do anything' for her if asked, also wrote about how she had been jealous of her as a child. This negatively experienced emotion was able to coexist with care, as well as ebbing over time (the ways these emotional facets of siblingship change over time will be discussed in more detail in Chapter 5).

Being there for a sibling also involves crunch points when support is offered. In their exploration of how people work out whether to give help to a relative, Janet Finch and Jennifer Mason gave respondents a selection of hypothetical scenarios and asked them what they would do. They found that there were '*some circumstances* in which most people do agree that the family should take responsibility' (1993: 18, original emphasis). These were circumstances where the help needed was legitimate and the person deserving, where the time, effort or skill required was limited, or where help was given by parents to children. In the following discussion we see some of these features in the sort of help, particularly practical help, provided by siblings. However, there is something particular about siblingship, particularly in childhood, when it comes to crunch points where help is required and these relate to the backstage nature of siblingship (as identified by Punch, 2008) as opposed to more hierarchical relationships with parents. For example, though 'telling tales' about sibling misbehaviour to parents was a common source of irritation, young people and mass observers often recalled times when they stuck together in the face of parental punishment. In the following focus group discussion among 11–12 year olds at St Stephen's, we see how siblings can stick together even in the context of a relationship that is usually characterised by fighting or, in the case of the bowling ball incident, in response to an act of violence:

> Participant 1: Me and my sister, we normally fight at home, but if she's like in trouble I'll help her.

> Participant 2: If we break something at home, like me and my brother'll just say we'll say one of us just walked past it and it dropped.

> …

> Participant 3: My brother dropped a bowling ball on my foot and … I just said it rolled off.

The material experience of being there changes, of course, post childhood, when siblings who had shared a home might move away and relationships are often navigated across geographical distance. However, many mass observers wrote about the importance of having a sibling in adulthood who can be there as a source of support during tough times, such as illness or divorce. Being there in adulthood sometimes meant regular contact – and many mass observers wrote about the ways they kept in touch – but this was not always the case, and others describe caring and supportive relationships that featured little or sporadic contact. The following examples from mass observers' accounts indicate some of these ways that siblings care for one another in adulthood.

Contact as care

One 58-year-old man (C4988) wrote fondly about his brother and sister, with whom he has what he characterises as a 'good' relationship featuring 'constant contact, in person as well as by text, phone and email'. Significantly, this man contacts his sister more regularly than his brother because she lives alone, and he is aware that she requires emotional support following the death of her partner. So here, regular contact is part of the way he responds to his sister's need for care as well as how he maintains his positive sibling relationships.

A 61-year-old woman (H1745) similarly wrote about providing care through contact, and her self-described 'timely' response to the Mass Observation directive was written seventeen days after the death of her sister's husband. The observer commented that she had seen her sister more in the previous few weeks than in the previous three years: 'Since my sister's husband died, I've been trying to make sure I talk to her every day (or at least every other day) on the telephone. I can't do much to help but I think it makes a big difference if people keep in touch.' Interestingly, this mass observer also wrote that she and her husband had offered financial help for private medical care, but this was never taken up by her sister. Though it was important that the offer was made, care in the form of regular contact was most meaningful and helpful. In these two examples, contact is a valued aspect of the sibling relationship and is how these individuals care for their siblings, increasing contact in response to need – in the crisis situation of the second observer's sister's recent bereavement and in response to the vulnerability of the first observer's sister.

Practical and emotional care and the meaning of siblingship

A 39-year-old mass observer (G2776) wrote about more practical help that she has provided to her brother. She defines this help as evidence that she has been a 'good big sister over the years' and describes actions relating to her older age, such as babysitting him when their parents were on holiday and then driving him to join them so he did not have to miss out on a party that weekend, as well as providing support when he was revising for his A level exams in the form of a 'pep talk'. In describing this help as synonymous with being a good sister, this respondent is reflecting on what a sibling is and should be in terms of the provision of care. Another 82-year-old respondent (H260) talked more explicitly about how care defines siblingship, reflecting upon the support she provided to her brother when he got divorced and comparing this to relationships with friends who, she writes, 'often let you down and cannot always be trusted with confidential things'.

In both these examples we see the idea that there is something special about the sibling relationship in terms of providing help and support (here gender is perhaps part of the emotional support provided, and the 39-year-old mass observer describes the emotional help given 'as a sister'), yet we also see the significance of the quality and nature of the relationship. This echoes Finch and Mason's finding that 'offers of help [between kin] do not follow straightforwardly from the genealogical relationship' (1993: 164); rather 'a sense of responsibility for helping someone else *develops* over time, through interaction between the individuals involved' – thus these responsibilities are created within live relationships (1993: 167, original emphasis).

Of course, sibling relationships are not always characterised by care. F3641, a 71-year-old mass observer, wrote about being grateful that she is an only child because of the difficulties she has witnessed her husband facing with his sibling relationships, which have involved conflict over an inheritance, alcohol and financial difficulties and which she describes as aggravating her husband's eczema and affecting his health.

Sibling relationships that lacked care were also described by young people. In the following example, Adam (a 12-year-old white British boy interviewed at the rural youth club) is responding to being asked about the advantages and disadvantages of being the youngest in the family by describing how his older brother and sister treat him:

Adam: Terror. You just get bullied.

Interviewer: You get bullied?

Adam: No, no I don't mean, like, in that way, I mean I'm like their slave. [in a shouty voice] 'Go and make me a cup of tea.'

This is perhaps where the co-presence that characterises many sibling relationships differs from Brownlie's account of 'being there'. Siblingship is unique in that being there as emotional care is not always present or acknowledged. As I have written elsewhere (Davies, 2019), building on Carol Smart's (2007) account of the stickiness of relationships, sibling relationships are 'sticky' in that they continue to matter, informing self and identity and feeling like a significant tie, even when not experienced as positive. Help and care can still be experienced as an almost taken-for-granted by-product of the sibling relationship. We have seen that sibling relationships can be characterised by a combination of irritation, annoyance and care. Following David Morgan's (1996) concept of family practices as ways of doing siblingship, we can understand these combinations as what Edwards and colleagues (2006: 60) term 'sibling practices' and what Wentzel Winther and colleagues (2015a) term 'conflictual closeness'. In the following section I take forward the idea of doing siblingship to consider what makes a sibling.

Sibling-like relationships and the importance of doing siblingship

People can become sisters or brothers when not related by blood or marriage as a result of the nature of the relationship becoming sibling-like. Similarly, step- or half-siblings can be understood as 'real' siblings or not depending on whether they are characterised by sibling practices, in other words whether they *do* siblingship (Morgan, 1996). The things that makes a relationship a sibling relationship are, of course, variable, but the idea of longevity, of growing up together and sharing some element of childhood is strongly associated with siblingship.

In the following example, Sofia (a 13-year-old mixed-race girl interviewed at Highfields), who has one sister, two step-siblings (one step-brother, one step-sister) and two half-siblings (one half-sister, one half-brother), is discussing her different relationship with her full, half- and step-siblings:

> Sofia: It's like really complicated. Cos I live with my mum and stepdad and I've got a sister who's got the same mum and dad, my younger sister in Year 7. And I've got, erm, my mum's husband's got two children, Maisie and Jay, and Maisie's like one of my best friends ... we're really close.

> Interviewer: Is she your age?

> Sofia: Erm, she's sixteen, she's just left school. And, erm, my dad's got, me dad's got me and my little sister and then I've got another

older sister and an older brother that he had before he met my mum. So I've got half a sister. And then my dad's got a new girlfriend [laughs] so he's got, so there's like these two girls but they're not really like, I wouldn't call them sisters.

Interviewer: Oh, right, okay. So you're not quite so close with them?

Sofia: No, cos they're dead young as well, they're like seven and ten.

It is clear that what makes Sofia's siblings feel like siblings is more complex than how they are related in terms of connection by blood or marriage, and this is reminiscent of Jennifer Mason and Becky Tipper's (2008) emphasis on children's creativity in working out their kinship ties. The connection Sofia is describing comes from the quality of the relationship – her feelings of closeness and friendship with Maisie – as well as the fact that her father's girlfriend's daughters cannot (yet) be called sisters because they are too young. Not only has there not been time to form a relationship with sibling qualities but the age gap means that they have not shared their childhoods in a way commonly associated with siblingship. Hayley Davies (2012), in her study of children's relationships, similarly found that children who had minimal contact with half- and step-siblings and who had not lived with these relatives experienced fewer opportunities for knowing and maintaining these relationships. Drawing on John Urry's (2002) concept of co-presence, Davies (2015) goes on to discuss the importance of physical proximity between siblings for building intimacy, emphasising the importance of touch, physical play and bodily contact in children's sibling relationships. Gulløv, Palluden and Wentzel Winther (2015) also point to the literal physical friction between siblings in their analysis. This is echoed in the account of a 24-year-old mass observer (C4271) who wrote that she considers herself an only child because she did not meet her two step-sisters until she was 19 or 20 years old: 'I did not grow up with siblings and I still don't really consider myself to have any … We were all adults with our own lives before we became "siblings".'

In the same way that it can be common for siblings not to *feel* 'real' if they do not have this essence of shared childhood, others described relationships that came to be sibling relationships due to this sharing. A 47-year-old mass observer (C3691), for example, wrote of her 'unofficially adopted' younger brother, telling the story of how he met her mother and asked her to be his adoptive grand-mother. The story of the development of a sibling relationship between the two highlights the importance of sharing elements of everyday life: 'I then got to know him as he was often at Mum's house, and we used to cook Chinese meals together.' The woman wrote, 'We just adopted each other as brother and sister with no fuss' and depicts the help they give one another (practical help with moving home, emotional support following a marriage breakdown) as evidence of their sibling-like relationship. In their exploration of transnational adoption in Norway and Spain, Signe Howell and Diana Marre (2006) emphasise the work done by adoptive parents to 'kin' their children, highlighting discursive practices undertaken such as emphasising resemblances with the adopted child and telling stories about the matching process whereby children are matched to their adoptive parents. Howell and Marre note that the obvious racial difference between adoptive parents and their children represents 'an enigma to the ignorant outside eye, a challenge to the normal order of things' (2006: 309). As with Janet Finch's concept of display, where displaying the fact that actions are indeed 'family' practices takes on heightened significance in situations where the diversity and fluidity of family forms mean that the 'contours and character' of family 'are not obvious' (2007: 73), these practices of kinning are heightened in importance because relatedness cannot be easily 'read' from family practices. We see similar kinning work in the mass observer's account of her relationship with her 'brother', with kinship ties created and displayed through their actions, such as when the mass observer's 'brother' made her his daughter's godmother, creating an avenue into an official 'named' family tie. As with Howell and Marre's parents, the observer also points to a physical resemblance between her and her 'brother': '[He] has red hair too, so it is easy for people to believe that we really are related, although when mum says he's her grandson it gets complicated!'

   This kinning work is a direct contrast to the taken-for-granted, background nature of the forms of being there described in the previous section, which are not displayed and instead lie dormant for much of the time. Alyson Rees and Andrew Pithouse explored birth children's experiences of living in foster families, demonstrating how 'sibling-like' relationships and practices were negotiated, judged and worked at over time: 'While every birth and foster child is unique, they none the less share in a relational process that requires both to negotiate a complex set of identities, settings, meanings and actions' (2019: 374). The emphasis on the process, work and skill that is invested in a relationship becoming sibling-like is significant, revealing the agency involved in forming new sibling-like relationships.

A sense of a shared childhood was not always necessary for a relationship to become sibling-like when other sibling practices are present. One 61-year-old mass observer (H1745) included in her directive a section headed 'My Sister' to describe her blood sister and one entitled 'My "brother"' to describe a man she thinks of as her brother. This 'brother' is a Moroccan man who stayed with her and her partner after his divorce, and began calling her partner 'brother'. Here we see a sibling relationship born out of emotional care, and perhaps this story reflects differing cultural norms around naming someone 'my brother' and the meaning of 'brother' being more than blood in some contexts. In the UK, for example, worth and a feeling of permanence can be endowed on a friendship by declaring a friend to be 'like a sister' or 'like a brother'. Similarly, value can be added to sibling relationships by stating that one's sibling is one's 'best friend'.

These uses of the language of siblingship can have heightened importance in different cultural contexts. In her study of African-Caribbean family relationships, Mary Chamberlain points to the metaphor of siblings as 'a cohort that will embrace both kinship and friendship networks' (2006: 169). Metaphors of siblingship, of being 'like sisters' or 'like brothers', were particularly important in the early stages of migration when trust and support between friends on arrival in the UK were crucial. Chamberlain writes:

> Networks were put to work to survive in a context of social and racial exclusion, integrating material help, social support and cultural identity. But they did so in a particular way, through the relationships of lateral kin and friendships and through the language of collectivity. (2006: 170)

Thus we see that siblings are made by far more than genetics. Following Morgan (1996), we can understand the importance of practices of care – such as the provision of practical and emotional support – that are also culturally understood as 'family' things. We also see the role of annoyance in both lived and discursive facets of siblingship, and this coexistence of annoyance and care is part of what makes sibling relationships different from other relational forms. Furthermore, we have seen that siblingship is not always actively practised or displayed but can take the form of a feeling of being there that can be largely dormant. So far I have discussed this 'being there' mainly in terms of emotional and practical care. In the following section I move the discussion on to the embodied, physical characteristics of many people's sibling relationships, particularly in childhood.

Embodied closeness: sensory and material affinities

> We sense others. We know what they are like and who they are by seeing, touching, smelling, hearing and generally experiencing the sensations of them, at the same time as they are experiencing the sensations of us. (Mason, 2018: 7)

Mason argues for the importance of attending to sensations in our analyses of relationships, attuning to how relationships are 'felt, perceived and experienced in "the body"' as well as how 'they emanate and flow in things that happen, and things coming into contact' (2018: 7). Sibling relationships are particularly imbued with sensations. Mason builds on research conducted with Becky Tipper (Mason and Tipper, 2008) about children's understanding of kinship to explore the 'intimate sensory-kinaesthetic knowledge' (Mason, 2018: 27) that children have of their relatives, with 'real fighting' and 'play fighting' between siblings as a key example of this (2018: 26). Building on Mason's (2008) earlier work on 'sensory affinities', Hayley Davies (2015) also points to the ways in which the everyday co-presence of siblingship can enhance sensory knowledge of siblings, with sibling relationships characterised by embodied and inter-physical experiences. In this section I draw on these ideas about the physical and sensory characteristics of sibling interactions and the sensations of affinity that circulate between siblings to unpack the importance of the physicality of siblingship. From fighting to an embodied or sensory closeness which, like 'being there', is not necessarily characterised by overt physical affection but rather a more mundane, background presence, embodied sensations are a key part of why and how siblings matter.

In the extract below we see how the day-to-day irritations of 11-year-old friends Poppy, Abigail and Georgia's sibling relationships are mediated by their physicality. Their discussions of the ups and downs of their sibling relationships and birth-order positions are interspersed with descriptions of physical fights with their siblings and the role of their physical size in the reactions of their parents to these incidents of physical conflict:

> Poppy: No, it's rubbish being the oldest because you always get asked to do something, and say like… [overlapping]
>
> Abigail: [overlapping] And although it's, like, the younger brother or sister's fault, like, I always, er, my brother always, like, colours at the table and paints, and leaves glue and glitter and all that, and I always get asked to clean it up.
>
> Poppy: And my mum says like, 'Go do this,' and I'm like, 'Why can't Tilly do it?' and she goes, 'Cos you're older.' And say, like, the computer broke, then I'll get, say, she'll say it's my fault cos I'm older.
>
> Abigail: And then they always believe…
>
> Georgia: [overlapping] She'll do the sweet face sort of thing.
>
> Abigail: [overlapping] And then, like, if your brother or your sister hits you first, starts hitting you, and you're like ignoring it, and at one point you just, like, smack them as hard as you can and tell them to stop, I always get in trouble saying, 'Well, you shouldn't smack him.'
>
> Poppy: My mum goes [puts on mock distressed voice] 'You're twice the size of her.' [giggles]
>
> Abigail: Although, like, they've been doing it to us. [overlapping]
>
> Georgia: Poppy, you're really tall so it's three times cos your [sister is] tiny.
>
> [all white British and interviewed together at the rural youth club]

Here we see how physical violence is discussed as part of a myriad of annoying things about being the oldest sibling, and the sensory kinaesthetics of siblingship are part and parcel of the everyday experiences of birth order. The size difference between these children and their younger siblings is also used to enhance their culpability by parents and, it seems, is played up by their younger siblings in performing their 'sweet face'. Though manifesting around negative practices (hitting), this discussion is indicative of a physical and embodied closeness lived by younger siblings in their day-to-day lives, and we see the embodied ways in which relationships are made sense of by others.

Mason, a 13-year-old boy, does not have any siblings at home, yet his imaginings of what sharing a home with brothers and sisters would be like are shaped by his understandings of fighting as a taken-for-granted part of siblingship:

> Mason: Erm [the advantages of not having siblings at home are] I have the four bedrooms to myself. Erm, I get more, like, attention off my mum than if there was a few of us. But the disadvantages is that, like, sometimes you get a bit bored on your own. And, like, say it's raining, none of your mates are playing out or anything, you get bored just sat in on your own, like. But there is another advantage, when I always go round to Sammy's house, him and his sister are always fighting, they never stop fighting. But I don't have anyone to fight with so that's, I think that's why I'm like I am because I don't, like, fight that much and think that I've never had a brother to, like, fight with or anything.

Mason's reflections on not having siblings centre quite heavily on the material and embodied elements that he understands as being central to sibling relationships. The physical fights he has witnessed his friends having with their siblings are entwined in his imaginings of everyday life as a sibling. His ambivalence about not having anyone to fight with derives from the inseparability of physical altercations from other advantages and disadvantages of being and having siblings.

The embodied closeness that characterises many sibling relationships is also present in Ed's description of his relationship with his sister – the size difference and physicality between them is an important component of their relationship, in terms of touch (picking her up and dropping her) and in terms of using his larger size to exercise control of where she can go in the house:

> Ed: I just like, so I can pick her up and drop her, and she can only get into the tree if the ladders are down or, if she gets on the bins, so I knock over the bins, er, bring up the ladders so she can't get up, and now she wants to get up so instead I just swing down and she can't get down…

These examples see a kind of tangling of physical conflict with the day-to-day annoyances and irritations of siblingship. Of course, physical violence is a common feature of many sibling relationships in childhood, and Edwards and colleagues point to children's own constructions of conflict with their siblings as part of their general 'annoyingness', as well as a cultural construction of parents as ultimately responsible for the 'civilisation' of their children. Edwards and colleagues go on to use their psycho-dynamic framework to situate aggression as a 'normal, although widely varying, feature of people's internal dynamics and relationships with others' (2006: 91) without denying the potential for sibling aggression to be damaging and abusive. Indeed, Amy Meyers (2017) points to the lack of distinction between day-to-day sibling aggression and abuse, making it difficult for practioners to support families. Here I want to focus on conflict as part of what Mason terms the 'sensory-kinaesthetic register' (2018: 9), considering how the enhanced physicality of sibling relationships can help us to attune to the embodied, sensory elements of relationality which sociologists often overlook.

The embodied, sensory closeness of childhood siblingship was recalled by a number of mass observers. One (G4466), for example, had a baby brother who had died at five months old, and wrote of still having 'a sensation' of the smell of the top of his head. G3655 had similar sensory and embodied memories of his older sisters, remembering them, and specifically their physical closeness expressed through cuddling, through the smell of their clothes and the smells and tastes of the food they used to cook:

> My oldest sister served in the timber corps, a branch of the Woman's Land Army. I was only four years old, but I remember the smell of her damp greatcoat when she gave me a cuddle when on leave.

> She would make cream toffee, cinder toffee and toffee cakes. I would be sent to bed. When they thought I was asleep they would make chips for their supper: I would smell the fragrant smell of frying chips, and would yell down the stairs, 'You're making chips!' I would often get a small portion on a plate in bed.

In her discussion of sensations of affinity, Mason argues for an understanding of sensations which moves beyond practices to account for the ways people are 'wondering – but also remembering, conjuring and animating, in ways that were full of sensations' (2018: 54). Here we see the centrality of sensation in the ways that this man, himself now in later life, conjures memories of his sisters that are imbued with sensations of smell, touch, feeling, taste and kinaesthesia, and are central to the *experience* of his sibling relationships.

This chapter has so far explored some of the experiences of being and having brothers and sisters. In pointing to common characteristics of siblingship such as physical proximity, it has been possible to push concepts such as 'care' and 'being there' to incorporate the coexistence of positive aspects of care with annoyance, and the embodied sensations of being there. In so doing this chapter has illuminated the significance of the day-to-day context of siblingship in childhood. In the following section I pick up the idea that sibling-ship can be done differently in different contexts, with both the practices of siblingship and the sensations of how siblingship *feels* differing across contexts.

Doing siblingship and being a sibling in context

The contexts in which siblingship is done are important for the ways that the ups and downs of sibling relationships are experienced. In the previous section I demonstrated how the proximate nature of sibling relationships can be experienced at once as a form of emotional care ('living alongside') and physical aggression and conflict. Here I explore some of the ways that siblingship is lived in various contexts in order to tease out differences in the balance of these facets of siblingship in everyday life. I consider how the sibling relationship is lived and performed in the context of home, often understood as 'backstage'; the more formal context of school where children are organised by age; the context of out-of-school clubs where siblings can be a source of support; and the role of the local community, as explored by Edwards and colleagues (2006). In exploring these different contexts, it is possible to see how sibling practices shift and adapt to different environments and how the meanings of siblingship can change, particularly regarding birth order and what it means to be the oldest, middle or youngest sibling in different situations.

Home

In her Goffmanian analysis of siblingship as a particularly backstage relationship, Punch (2005) focuses on how siblings engage in backstage behaviours such as fighting. Many of these practices take place in the home, which is often seen as a 'backstage' space where less formal presentations of self are possible. As alluded to in the previous section, sharing space with siblings at home can be challenging, and the enforced togetherness that it can create was a key feature of many accounts of sibling relationships, from young people's descriptions of their everyday lives with their siblings to memories of childhood homes shared by mass observers. Yet growing up in close physical proximity can be an important part of the experience of siblingship (H. Davies, 2015) and can create the 'conflictual closeness' identified by Wentzel Winther and colleagues (2015a).

Sharing a bedroom was a key challenge for many people, and a number of mass observers had strong childhood memories of this. One 70-year-old man (D1602) remembered drawing imaginary lines to separate sections of the bedroom he shared with his older brother. Similarly, an 80-year-old mass observer (H1805) recalled hearing his sisters, who had the smallest room in the house and shared a double bed, quarrelling through the bedroom wall at night. Jade, a 12-year-old white British girl who attended St Stephen's school, talked in her interview about having her own bedroom following an attic conversion at her father's house. Jade was grateful that her siblings could no longer make a mess in her room and that she could control the television she had in there. However, she also talked about missing aspects of sharing with her younger brother: 'If you make a mess you have to tidy it up. You can't just leave it. And you get kind of bored sometimes like and you don't have no one to speak to.' The idea that, even if sometimes too close for comfort, the heightened proximities of sharing a home with one's sibling(s) afford a particular kind of 'living alongside' is important. Take the following quote from 12-year-old Adam: 'Well my older, older sister is in university, so she's, like, got her own house so I don't really see her, but my er younger of the two sisters I get on with, I mess about with her.' The notion of 'messing about' is significant and describes the backstage-style sibling relationship identified by Punch (2005) as characterising sibling relationships.

Of course, the concept of home is not always straightforward. In their exploration of sibling children of divorced parents, Wentzel Winther and colleagues identify the significance of time spent 'in-between' spaces as siblings travel between homes, identifying the centrality of packing, unpacking and carrying bags. Here being 'in-between' meant both physically commuting as well as spending time 'between different ways of *doing home* and being siblings' (2015a: 66).

School

Young people often share the same school with their siblings, and the ways that siblingship is done at school can seem to be quite contradictory. Many young people in interviews and focus groups described a feeling of responsibility for providing support to their sibling at school. Work emanating from the Families and Social Capital ESRC Research Centre emphasises these practices of care and indicates how siblings (particularly older siblings) can provide information about school as well as emotional and social support (Holland, 2008), offer specific support in dealing with bullying (Hadfield et al., 2006) and generate social capital even where sibling relationships are conflictual (Gillies and Lucey, 2006).

At the same time, many young people in my study described a different day-to-day relationship with their siblings in the more public arena of school, where they often avoided one another and felt embarrassed by their sibling's presence, perhaps because they represented a blurring of the boundaries between home and school, between frontstage and backstage performances of identity. The differences in these performances are summed up in this description of an 11-year-old focus group participant's brother's behaviour at home and school:

> Erm they act hard in front of their mates and they'll try and show off in front of them like and in the house they'd like cry onto you and then outside, when they walk past you they'll go, 'Move', you know or something. [St Stephen's]

Here the child's description of the changes in his brother's behaviour at home and school quite clearly echoes Goffman's descriptions of different performances of the self in the frontstage arena of school, where the audience of friends and peers necessitates the shows of bravado described by his brother, a contrast to the displays of vulnerability that are possible at home.

It was common for young people to reflect on trying to avoid their siblings at school or feeling embarrassed upon encountering them during the school day, an indication of the discomfort of being confronted with their backstage selves while in front of an audience. Take the following focus group discussion among 13–14-year-olds at Highfields:

> Ryan: I used to talk to her out of school and I was like.
>
> Interviewer: OK. What about in school?
>
> Participant: I would be so embarrassed if my brother…
>
> Lauren: It's embarrassing.
>
> Maleehah: I would not. If my older brother or sister came here I would be like 'I don't know you.'
>
> Reece: When my little brother talks to my friends I just like tell him to go away I just hate him.

Similar views were expressed in the following focus group of 14–15-year-olds at the same school. Not everyone in this discussion spoke negatively about their siblings, but the idea that school is not a place where they can express positive feelings towards their brothers and sisters is emphasised:

> Mark: I've got a younger brother here [at school] and I just like, I smile at him but I'd never dream of like going up and speaking to him!
>
> [laughter.]
>
> Interviewer: And do you like walk to school with your brothers and sisters or…?
>
> Sadia: No!
>
> Participant: No!
>
> [laughter.]
>
> Interviewer: Why not do you think?
>
> Matthew: Embarrassed.
>
> Shelley: It's embarrassing!

[laughter.]

...

Matthew: Not really [embarrassing]. I like him. I do talk to him but not that much in school, I don't really see him.

Here we see that school is a context where, in contrast to home, young people often try to avoid being in close proximity with their brothers and sisters.

This does not mean that siblings cannot be a source of support in this context, and as Lucy Hadfield, Ros Edwards and Melanie Mauthner (2006) point out, most sibling relationships of support lie dormant at school, to be activated only when needed. Take 13-year-old Chanelle's descriptions of how she relates to her older brother at school:

> Chanelle: Because we're both, in front of our friends, like say, if one of us said 'Hiya' or something, we'd just ignore each other... Or we'd ... just say 'Shut up' or something... Whereas when we're at home we actually do speak.
>
> Interviewer: If you were having a problem at school, would you have gone to your brother even though you weren't that...?
>
> Chanelle: Yeah, I would have gone to my brother if I was having a problem in school and, like, I'd tell him about it ... because he's older than me and he's probably been through it before, then he'd know some advice to give me.
>
> [white British, interviewed at holiday club]

Here we see differences between the physical co-presence of siblingship as lived at home and the common desire for distance in the more 'frontstage' arena of school, though the idea that siblings are 'there' if needed remains.

Holiday club

Unlike at school where many siblings maintain a physical distance from one another, siblings tended to 'stick together' in out-of-school holiday clubs. Holiday clubs offer childcare and activities for school-age children in the school holidays. They are commonly used in the UK during the six-week summer holidays as well as at Easter,

Christmas and half-term holidays. Holiday clubs offer a range of different activities and can be focused on sports, crafts, music and so on. I conducted some participant observation for a week in the summer of 2007 in a holiday club in the UK where young people between the ages of 6 and 14 took part in various arts and crafts activities. In this section I share some of my observations of the ways siblings interacted during the week, along with conversations I had with siblings at the club. In so doing I unpack some of the contradictions and complexities of doing siblingship in this context, drawing attention to the ways siblings supported each other at the club, not as a dormant safety net to be activated when needed, like in school, but as an active source of support and company in an unfamiliar setting which older siblings were able to benefit from as much as younger siblings. Coupled with this I explore the ways that older siblings at the same time experience heightened responsibility for their younger brothers and sisters in this context.

Sticking together – siblings as a source of mutual support

In stark contrast to the avoidance techniques many young people described using at school, most children at the holiday club stuck with their sibling (and in some cases cousin(s)), particularly in the first few days when the club was unfamiliar and they had not yet got to know other people there. As 12-year-old Naomi stated of coming to the holiday club with her younger brother, 'For about a week he'll be with me when I, while I try and make other friends, but after a week he'll do his own thing.'

I noticed that siblings would tend to eat lunch together and opt for the same activities when offered a choice. Though some siblings did separate towards the end of the week once they started to make friends with other children of their own age, I noticed younger siblings being incorporated into these new friendship groups. The separation between friends and siblings seen at school was not present in this context. Though some of the young people at the club had cousins and friends present, they did not stick together as closely as with their siblings. Sometimes this sticking together involved the older child taking responsibility for looking after their younger sibling. For example, the lunchtime assistant told me about two sisters who were walking into the lunch room the previous day when the younger sister slipped and banged her head. The lunchtime assistant and other members of staff rushed over to see if the child was hurt but the older sister would not let them examine or talk to her. Instead she spoke for her sister while holding her close, answering the staff's questions on her behalf. Obviously here the older sister felt some responsibility for looking after her sister after her accident, but this example seems to be about more than just responsibility; the older sister knew that in an unfamiliar environment like the holiday club her sister would be better comforted by her sibling than by staff members she didn't know well.

Having a sibling at the holiday club could be a comfort for older siblings too. 13-year-old Joseph, for example, had obvious feelings of responsibility for his younger brother Anis (which I discuss in the following section), but he also spoke of the benefits of attending the workshops with his brother, saying that coming to holiday club was 'better as a pair' because 'if you don't make friends on the first day, I've got my brother as well'. Here Anis's company provides Joseph with a safety net – guaranteed companionship that means he will never be alone during holiday club.

Being responsible

Though sticking together with siblings provided comfort and companionship, it also gave a heightened level of responsibility for older siblings who, despite the presence of adult carers, acted *in loco parentis* in the holiday club setting. Watching the young people arrive and register for their sessions, I was struck by how many children were brought along by an older sibling who registered both themselves and their younger sibling on arrival. Many of the older siblings also looked after the packed lunches for themselves and their sibling(s), sometimes a difficult and stressful task, with many children misplacing their lunchbox or finding it tiresome to keep with them.

For some brothers and sisters this sense of responsibility continued throughout the week. When, during different lunchtimes, I approached 13-year-old Estella (a black Caribbean girl who attended the club with her 5-year-old sister, Alesha) and Joseph (mentioned above, a 13-year-old white Albanian and British boy who attended the club with his 5-year-old brother Anis) about taking part in their interview, both commented that, despite the fact that the lunch break was supervised by members of staff, they could not leave their younger sibling. They also continued to take responsibility for their younger sibling during the interview and both felt it necessary to step in to ensure that they engaged appropriately with the interaction as well as monitoring their behaviour:

> Interviewer: And what about you Alesha, have you been having a nice time?
>
> [pause – Alesha starts dipping her fingers in various paint and glue pots left in the room]
>
> Interviewer: Don't put your fingers in those. They'll make you messy. Have you been having fun, Alesha?
>
> [pause]
>
> Estella: [to Alesha] You have to speak!

In fact, keeping an eye on Alesha during my short interview with Estella (which I eventually had to cut short because of the need to keep Alesha entertained) was a constant battle, and as well as answering my questions and engaging in the interview herself, Estella had to repeatedly advise Alesha about how to use the paints, warn her not to run out of the room and generally try to supervise her. This behaviour is also interesting because Estella's feelings about Alesha are ambivalent to say the least; she described her as 'loud' and 'a bit boasty', and visibly scowled when the lunchtime assistant told her she thought they looked alike. Estella used to come to the holiday club on her own (primarily to attend drama workshops) but Alesha had recently started coming too because she also enjoyed some of the activities. It seems that, despite the burden of responsibility this places on Estella, she saw Alesha's presence at the club as potentially helping to improve the quality of their relationship:

> Interviewer: So what's it like coming with your sister as opposed to just on you own?
>
> Estella: Erm, a bit of a pain cos she likes to always be there but, erm, it's okay, it's nice to build a bond.

Joseph's little brother Anis, although the same age as Alesha, sat quietly at Joseph's side for the majority of his interview. However, Joseph's sense of responsibility for Anis's conduct in the interview was similar to Estella's. Not only could he not leave Anis in the lunch room while he took part in the interview but he also felt that he needed to step in and make sure that Anis 'does well' in the interview and answered the questions 'correctly'. After talking with Joseph about his favourite school subjects, I asked Anis what he enjoyed at school:

Anis: Guitar's the favourite and...

Joseph: [overlapping] No. What do you like doing most?

Anis: Playing on the Nintendo Wii.

[interviewer laughs]

Joseph: [sighs] At school!

Anis: At school? Playing at school.

Joseph: No, what work are you good at?

Anis: Maths and reading.

Joseph: [to interviewer] Reading.

Here Joseph seems to see himself as a sort of broker for his younger brother, passing on my questions to him and persevering until he, on Anis's behalf, is able to provide me with an answer he deems satisfactory. Like Estella, he also demonstrates how much patience is necessary to attend a place such as the holiday club with a younger sibling (and no parent).

These observations highlight how siblingship is done differently in the less familiar context of the holiday club. Here, the practices of 'being there' resonate more closely with the emotional support outlined in Brownlie's (2014) exploration, and siblings were able to gain a sense of ongoing comfort and support from one another, irrespective of birth order. At the same time, a different sort of – more active – care passed exclusively from older to younger siblings in the form of practical parenting-type support such as keeping the lunchboxes, managing behaviour and dealing with injuries (in the case of the sisters I was told about, through embodied intimacies). Edwards and colleagues (2006) similarly point to the heightened responsibilities of older siblings in introducing younger siblings to hobbies and extracurricular activities, where they also found that older siblings often experienced heightened responsibilities, accompanying their brothers and sisters to sessions.

Locality and geographical distance

In the previous chapter I pointed to Edwards and colleagues' observation that siblingship is also done in spaces beyond the home, in the local community. The authors note how older siblings' experiences in the 'outside world' (2006: 106) influence their younger brothers and sisters and the responsibilities they felt they had for them, reminiscent of the feelings of responsibility I observed at the holiday club. Edwards and colleagues also note how 'sisters and brothers could be implicated heavily in the moral reputation of children and young people in the context of their neighbourhood' (2006: 106), and children in their study spoke of being embarrassed by the behaviour of siblings. At the same time, Edwards and colleagues discuss the 'defensive landscape of the neighbourhood' and the complexities of siblings 'sticking up for each other' in the community beyond the home (2006: 106). I too found that the protection that young people derived from older siblings in school carried over into the local area, and that this was particularly pronounced among the young people I interviewed who lived on the economically deprived housing estate and attended the youth club there. Here participants were embedded in a network of support spanning from their siblings, with siblings being a useful source of social capital on the estate as well as in contexts beyond. Thus solidarity was derived from siblings and the social networks they allowed access to in response to being associated with a stigmatised place.

Take the following example from the 14-year-old, white British Lois, in which she talks about the benefits she derives from her brother's friends:

> Lois: Yeah it is, cos you know that if anything like, any, like, person comes up to you and you don't know, you know they're going to stick up for you that night and you know that you can trust them because, like, or if you need to tell your brother something but you don't really want to tell him, you know you can tell, like, your brother's mate, and they'll tell him, like, but not, like, put it in a bad way, put it in, like, a good way across, so, we don't get in trouble as much. [laughs]

Here we see that Lois does not have to tell her brother directly if she needs him to 'stick up' for her because she can access his social networks and derive support from his friends.

While doing siblingship in the local area/community is an important part of the experience of siblingship in childhood, geographical distance is often a feature of sibling relationships later in the life course. A number of mass observers had siblings who had emigrated and often this meant that relationships became more distant, even when they had been close as children, particularly for those older observers whose siblings emigrated before internet correspondence was possible and when international phone calls were very expensive. Some observers reminisced about having played in the street together as children or being in more regular contact in the past. For other observers, even relatively short geographical distances meant a huge decline in contact with their siblings, particularly in later life. The taken-for-granted proximity of siblings in the contexts of home, school, holiday club and community in childhood often dissolve as geographical distance increases, and instead conscious work and effort needs to be expended to maintain the relationship.

Resemblances and magical affinities

Part of the reason why sibling relationships are so fascinating is that they represent some of the mysteries of relatedness. Siblings can resemble one another in appearance or characteristics in ways that seem unequivocally to demonstrate a connection, or they can be different in ways that seem unfathomable given shared upbringing or genes. Furthermore, connections between siblings can be uncanny or otherworldly in ways that confound sociological explanation. These aspects of siblingship mean that connections between siblings cannot be wholly explained through the frames of practices, care or identity, which are more familiar to sociologists of families and relationships. Mason addresses these connections in her discussion of what she terms the 'ineffable' nature of kinship: 'Some of the most potent affinities feel like an ineffable kinship; a *something* that is in connection, with a charge that feels fixed, immutable and elemental' (2018: 59, original emphasis). These connections can 'seem to have a sense of mystery at their very heart, which is hard to explain or put into words' (Mason, 2018: 59), so that connections can at once be fixed and undeniable while also somehow evading our comprehension. Mason discusses family resemblances as a facet of this ineffable kinship – as connections that can be given, fixed and evidential, grounded in genetic relatedness as well as mysterious, fleeting and uncanny, possessing what Mason describes as a 'haunting ethereal in/tangibility' (2018: 60). Mason urges social scientists to pay attention to resemblances and take them seriously as a meaningful facet of connection.

Resemblances certainly feature heavily in the meanings and experiences of siblingship. Think of the mass observer discussed earlier in this chapter who identified a resemblance with her non-genetic 'brother'; the resemblance was an outward physical sign of relatedness, creating siblingship in ways similar to couples in Petra Nordqvist's (2010) study of lesbian motherhood, for whom resemblance was a way of emphasising connectedness between the baby and both mothers, concealing the role of the donor.

In the following example, Farhana (a 14-year-old British Pakistani girl interviewed at Highfields) is explaining how she resembles her sister. The fact that she is mistaken for her sister echoes Mason's identification of the sensory 'evidential' nature of resemblances:

> Interviewer: But what, what do you think it is about you that makes everybody think that you look similar? Can you see it yourself or do you not, or you not sure?
>
> Farhana: I'd say we do look similar but some people actually mistake us for each other.
>
> Interviewer: Really?
>
> Farhana: Yeah. But, erm, yeah, erm, I, well we're kind of like the same height about, yeah, erm, and we tend to like, we tend to like wear the same clothes you know style of clothes. So I think that's why you know people could get confused. But it's quite funny though because, erm, my neighbours mistake me for her. She works at, you know, [local] Tesco [supermarket] just up there, yeah, as a part time job. [overlapping] ... So they're like, 'Oh so how's work at Tesco?' and I was like, 'Okay I don't know I think you're talking about my sister' and they're like, 'Oh right sorry I thought you were your sister' I was like, 'Okay' [laughs]
>
> Interviewer: Do you quite like it that people think that you're like your sister or are you not sure what to make?
>
> Farhana: Well I don't like it or I don't really dislike it I just think it's quite funny. [laughs]

In this case, Farhana's resemblance to her sister cannot be denied and its evidential nature is what links Farhana to her sister in the wider community. It is a peculiar connection that Farhana seems neither to particularly welcome nor bemoan, but this does not matter because Farhana and her sister's relationship is there for all to see, whether they want it or not.

Others spoke of strong physical resemblances that were commented on by strangers, with one mass observer remembering that people used to mistake him and his brother for twins when they were very young. In other cases, people seem more keen to contrive and demonstrate a resemblance. One mass observer (G4466), for example, described how her and her sister were dressed in identical handmade clothes by their mother and she had 'fond memories of white smocks with tiny little red flowers on them'. Here clothing seems to have been a way for her mother to signify or display (Finch, 2007) her daughters' siblingship to the wider community.

These resemblances are all outward symbols of a sibling relationship visible in the wider community beyond the home. Significant resemblances are not limited to outward appearance and can be embodied, less tangible connections (see Mason, 2008; Mason and Davies, 2009). One mass observer (C4988) noticed small habits and mannerisms that he shares with his brother, with whom he describes having a close relationship. This observer recalled a meal when they were both playing with their placemats in the same way, and then both put their coats on to leave the house and then took them off again, both placing them in the boots of their separate cars before driving away. Despite being more fleeting, existing in a series of small movements, this kinaesthetic resemblance was also observable by others, and the observer commented that both his and his brother's wives noticed.

Just as the presence of resemblances can signify a sibling relationship, their absence can cast doubt on its existence. D1602, for example, a 70-year-old male mass observer, described how a lack of resemblance with his brother caused him to doubt their relationship:

> Even as boys we were different – in looks, in character and in likes and dislikes and I went through a phase when I was about fourteen of wondering whether one of us had been adopted, partly because neither of us greatly resembled either of our parents or their ways. But I know enough about nature now to know that this can often happen in families and these days both BB and I have enough

mannerisms, characteristics and traits of both parents to show that we are true siblings – and to be honest I have to say that I am pleased that I have one.

In these cases we see resemblance as an outward sign of related-ness between siblings. 12-year-old Britney summed this up in her interview while discussing her genetic link with her half-sister: 'it's my mum that's, that's in us all, that you can *see* that we're related' (my emphasis).

Relatedness between siblings is not always so observable, and siblingship can also be experienced as something less tangible and somehow otherworldly, including 'spooky' and 'uncanny' aspects of connection, described by Mason as 'ethereal affinities' (2008). In the following quotation, Ryan (a 12-year-old white British boy who attended St Stephen's and was interviewed in the home he shares with his mother, her partner and their baby – his half-sister) is cultivating a narrative of 'closeness' by likening himself to his baby sister Annabel. In doing so, he points to the importance of sensory affinities as well as ethereal connections. The role of touch in this process (including in the articulation of the narrative) is also clear:

Ryan: Erm, cos when I was a baby I used to be dead quiet and er Annabel's dead quiet as well... I want to be Annabel's first word...

...

Ryan: Erm, I can see it [a resemblance] in Annabel yeah ... she's robbed my ears. Cos er, you should really have, like, a joint there [reaches up and bends his ear], shouldn't you?

Interviewer: Oh right.

Ryan: But we haven't, that's ... I'll show you there [shows interviewer Annabel's ears].

Interviewer: Oh yeah.

Ryan: And both of ours are stuck together.

Mum: They've got very pointy ears.

...

Ryan: And she's got one elf one.

Interviewer: One elf one?

Ryan: She's got er, a round one and one elf.

Interviewer: Have you got a round one and an elf as well?

Ryan: No, I've just got two elfs.

Interviewer: Oh okay.

Here Ryan is likening himself to his baby sister in both developmental patterns and physical resemblance, though the physical resemblance he discusses is unlikely to serve as the sort of outward symbol of connection that Britney described, where her mother could be 'seen' in all her siblings, as it requires intimate knowledge to detect the presence or not of 'elf ears' and physical closeness and touch to ascertain how the ears bend. It is clear from the way Ryan talks about wanting to be his sister's first word that he yearns for a close relationship with Annabel, and he cultivates this closeness through carefully observing her development and taking it upon himself to notice links and similarities. This actually started before Annabel's birth when Ryan and his mother spotted images in her scan photographs (the Virgin Mary and Bob Marley), and it was also Ryan who spotted the elf ears. Ryan's observations indicate the importance of physical embodied characteristics in the affirmation of his relationship with Annabel, and this is clearly seen in the way he displays the resemblance in the interview (physically bending his own and Annabel's ears to demonstrate the likeness).

There is evidence of Mason's (2008) ethereal affinity here too, a kind of mysterious link demonstrated both by the idea of a shared 'freaky' bodily resemblance in the ears and in the 'visions' Ryan spots in the scan photos (which he showed me during the interview). In making the case for an 'ineffable kinship', Mason (2018) discusses how resemblances can be at once evidential while also being elusive and mysterious. She argues that, as well as pertaining to questions of 'bio-genetic connection', resemblances have a 'haunting ethereal in/tangibility' and it is the entanglement of both genetics and magic that forms what she terms the 'potencies of connection' that we see in Ryan's connection with baby Annabel. The ways these resemblances are revealed are also part of their ethereality. Not everyone can see Bob Marley or the Virgin Mary in the scan photographs, but that is okay because Ryan and his mother have a close affinity to the baby in the pictures and hence can see these apparitions. Similarly, the elf ears require physical demonstrations and careful guidance from Ryan to be seen. He is the expert. Mason describes these moments of perception in her discussion of how ethereal affinities manifest: 'It can emerge inexplicably in transitory flashes that are visual, sensory, based in feeling or familiarity, and certainly in perception. It is hard to describe, it is rather magical, yet it is part of the everyday and it is deeply fascinating' (2008: 38).

I conclude this chapter with one final example, this time pointing to the ethereal connection between siblings in the account of a 55-year-old mass observer (A2212) and her relationship with her older sister. Due to a fourteen-year age gap, this woman did not feel she knew her sister well, so she started to write to her when she was in her twenties in an effort to get to know her. She found lots of shared likes, dislikes and fears. Despite some hints of difficulties in their relationship (the observer commented that their mother used to emphasise that she thought her to be less intelligent than her sister), the respondent points to a set of uncanny coincidences which serve to emphasise the existence of a special connection:

> I have had a number of paranormal experiences concerning my sister. When her marriage broke down, I dreamed about this accurately before she wrote to our mother to explain what had happened. My husband, my mother and I had no idea that the marriage was in trouble ... Then some more odd things happened. One Christmas, my husband and I were choosing presents for family members, and I saw a little set of 'nesting' globes where one globe fits inside another, like Russian dolls, and it was rather unusual, hand painted with gold embellishments, so I bought it for my sister and we sent it to her in the post. The next day, her present to us came in the post, and to our surprise, it contained a little set of 'nesting' globes, exactly the same as those we had sent her! Our gift to her had crossed in the post with hers to us. This reminds me that something similar had already happened. When I was a child of around eight, I went with my parents to visit my sister, and on the way, we stopped to look in a shop, where there was a 'nesting' Russian doll in the window. I very much wanted this doll, but for some reason I cannot now remember, my parents refused to buy it, and we went on to my sister's house. She took us up to the bedroom to show us something ... and right there on the window ledge was a Russian doll, just like I wanted. I pointed this out and my sister picked it up and gave it to me saying, 'Oh yes, I got this for you.'

The observer goes on to list other strange 'coincidences' surrounding gifts that her sister had bought for her. Though she uses the word 'coincidence', it is clear that the observer thinks there is more to these instances than coincidence, and together they seem to represent a more meaningful connection, 'an affinity that exists and emanates from somewhere ethereal, between and beyond persons and gestures' (Mason, 2008: 38).

Conclusion

This chapter has highlighted some of the facets of sibling relationships, from care and everyday proximities to the role of practices in producing siblingship and the ways sibling relationships are lived in different contexts, the significance of physical fighting, embodied closeness, resemblances and sensory connections. Of course, there are a myriad of different ways that sibling relationships are lived and experienced, and it is not possible to map all of these. It is, however, possible to see how some of the particularities of sibling relationships reveal the complexities of kinship in terms of the coexistence of seemingly contradictory relationship characteristics; siblings can be annoying and caring while also being imbued with a literal, embodied, sensory, spatial and physical proximity.

Indeed, sibling relationships are a site where we see the tangling of genetic, sensory and social aspects of kinship. As I mentioned in the introduction, in her concept of 'merographic connections', Marilyn Strathern (1992: 72) sees English kinship in terms of parts and wholes, with kinship being part of society (kin names such as 'brother' and 'sister', for example, belong to the realm of society) as well as part of biology (the names of gametes, for example, belong to the realm of science). These parts which belong to different wholes mingle in kinship, which inherently contains a mix of the natural and social. I think that siblings can be a site where these minglings are particularly visible – where 'nature' and 'nurture' exist in a way that invites questions, poses mysteries and is endlessly fascinating (Mason, 2008). Thus, thinking with siblings encourages us to expand our sociological understandings of relationality, incorporating parts of different wholes, which may be rooted in scientific or magical realms as well as more commonly thought-of sociological areas of inquiry.

Chapter 4

Imagination

We do not just live with our sibling relationships, we also live with the *idea* of siblings. Sibling relationships are imbued with ideas, ideals and imagined connections. From often contradictory ideas about how siblingship ought to be done and what sibling roles should entail to lay theories about how being a sibling might affect the ways we 'turn out' in life, normative ideas about what sibling relationships should mean are a significant facet of siblingship in the global north. Of course, there are no universal ideas about what siblingship ought to look like, and our ideas about siblings are informed by a complex tangle of cultural norms, lived experience and interpretations of 'expert' discourse. Furthermore, these ideas are often contradictory, do not map neatly on to lived experiences of being and having siblings, and can be resisted throughout the life course. What matters here is that, despite the differences, complexities and ambivalences in our ideas about what siblingship ought to entail, these ideals inform the ways we make sense of ourselves and our relationships.

Though ideas about normativity and discursive levels of thought are central to sociological thinking, looking at siblings can be particularly fruitful for thinking through these ideas as applied to personal relationships. There are two reasons for this. First, siblingship is a bundle of contradictions. More scripted than other relationships (such as those with friends) but less scripted than legally bound relationships with parents, sibling relationships are intragenerational, yet birth order and age differences can be keenly felt. There are normative assumptions about the ethic of care and responsibility between siblings, yet siblingship is a relational form unique in the normative acceptance of arguments, and even violence, as a 'natural' by-product of the relationship – in childhood at least. These contradictions mean that there are often large gaps between idealised images of how siblingship ought to be done and the lived realities of being and having a sibling. Studying these gaps between imagined relational forms and the lived realities of relationships can illuminate some of the ways that normative ideas are made sense of and lived with in people's everyday personal lives.

Secondly, the fascination with how siblingship works (outlined in the introductory chapter of this book) and the idea that siblingship implicates the self (outlined in Chapter 2) means that normative ideas abound regarding the ways that particular configurations of siblingship may affect how we 'turn out' in life. Studying these ideas can help us to understand the role of imagined, yearned-for relationships and how they can live alongside reflexive narratives of how our sibling role (or 'only child' status) may have affected who we are and who we can be. Related to this fascination with how siblingship affects how we can turn out in life is the way that siblings invoke wider understandings about inheritance, nature and nurture, and can be used as something of a test case for thinking through how things are passed on in families. This means that sibling relationships can be a useful sociological lens through which to explore how lay expertise works in informing our identities and relationships, furthering our understandings of what it means to be related.

Of course, despite many people being inclined to seek them, there can be no simple rules that govern how siblings ought to turn out and how they ought to treat one another. This would obscure the complexities of many family forms. Birth-order positions, for example, might shift and evolve, and some young people with divorced or separated parents might be the oldest sibling in one parent's house but have older siblings when visiting their other parent. Some only children may in fact have cousins or friends who they grow up with 'like siblings', whereas some people may find that the age gap with their sibling is so big that they effectively grew up as an only child. Roles attached to gender and birth order are culturally specific, and other scholars have written, for example, about the interactions of gender and age in South Asian family roles and household structure (Bhopal, 1997; Dale et al., 2002) or about the sibling-like role of cousin, friend and community relationships in many Caribbean families (Chamberlain, 2006). Sibling roles are also mediated by class (Edwards et al., 2006); some people might find themselves occupying particular roles and responsibilities because of a sibling's disability (Meltzer, 2016); or they might adopt certain caring responsibilities brought about by family circumstances such as the death or disability of a parent. There are a myriad different ways that siblingship, and any sense of responsibility attached to this relationship, is lived, but despite these complexities, it is interesting that normative discourses, tropes and imaginings of siblingship tend to assume that it can follow rules, both in terms of behaviour and in terms of kinship rules about how we turn out as a sibling. Despite cultural differences in what these normative ideas are, it matters that sibling relationships are particularly imbued with normative ideas, and these features of siblingship mean that they can be a helpful lens in illuminating how normative-ideal relational forms are lived with.

Siblings we live by and with

Despite rarely mapping neatly on to people's lived experiences of being and having siblings, ideas about how siblings ought to behave towards one another are a key facet of siblinghood. These normative rules are scripted by gender, age and birth-order positions as well as being culturally and ethnically contextual. Though rules are often breached in day-to-day relationships, and may differ greatly in different sociocultural contexts, they make their way into people's imaginations as well as some behaviours. Indeed, sibling relationships are often idealised in popular culture, as outlined in the introduction. Furthermore, there are normative ideas about the roles and responsibilities of siblings, and the idea of normative birth-ordered and gendered sibling roles is prominent in many cultural depictions of sibling relationships. Think of Jane Austen's *Pride and Prejudice*, in which the two older Bennett sisters are depicted as sensible role models, often acting *in loco parentis* for their silly younger sisters, or the juxtaposition of Elinor's 'sense' to her younger sister Marianne's 'sensibility' in Austen's novel *Sense and Sensibility*. The trope of the 'responsible' older sibling prevails in countless novels, plays, films and television programmes.

Similarly, sibling relationships are highly idealised in similar ways to relationships with friends or parents but have important differences. Unlike relationships with friends – which are often characterised as positive relationships of choice between equals (Smart et al., 2012; Heaphy and Davies, 2012) – or parents – characterised by a strong ethic of care and responsibility (Finch and Mason, 1993) – siblings are often expected to provide some support and care and to be something of a 'role model' for one another, while at the same time the relationship is more equal in terms of power than intergenerational relationships with parents (Punch, 2005). We see this in the way that likening other relationships to sibling relationships ('she's like a sister to me') lends them a sense of heightened intimacy, permanence and value. As explored in the previous chapter, siblingship may also be characterised by a close intimacy, while simultaneously occupying the unique role of a relationship in which it is deemed 'normal' to argue, compete and even physically fight with one another (Edwards et al., 2006; H. Davies, 2015). The tangling of these different – often contradictory – norms, discourses and imaginings of what siblingship is and should be make siblings a fruitful case for thinking through some of the contradictions and complexities in how discursive and moral norms are lived with, both in our everyday relationships and in our imaginings of alternative relational realities.

One of the key normative ideas about how siblings ought to behave, which is firmly attached to birth order, is that older siblings ought to be a role model for their younger brothers and sisters. The enhanced responsibilities attached to older sibling roles were touched on in the previous chapter, and are often seen, particularly by young people, as a disadvantage of being an older sibling. These roles are particularly potent during childhood and young adulthood, and many mass observers described sibling relationships later in the life course that seemed less structured by birth order, at least in terms of the exchange of help and support, though the idea that their birth-order position had influenced the way they had turned out in life was still significant, and I discuss this later in this chapter. Janet Finch and Jennifer Mason (1993), in their study of family responsibilities, also note how adult siblings expected the help and support they provided to be reciprocated. For example, help with childcare was always accompanied by a sense that the same favour would be reciprocated at some time in the future. There was no sense of older siblings expecting to give support that was not reciprocated. For young people, however, birth order can be hugely important, and the idea that 'big' siblings have responsibility and are meant to be role models for their younger siblings was commonly held by young people in interviews and focus groups. Though some older siblings were happy enough to take on this role, they did not always have much choice in the matter.

In an interview with three 12-year-old friends (all white British and interviewed at the rural youth club) – Abigail, Georgia and Poppy – Poppy began to discuss how annoying she found it when her younger sister copies her:

> Poppy: Oh that's what annoys me, she copies me and that ... If I start, like, wearing some type of trousers, she'll want to buy them and if I do like a squiggly 'y' when I'm doing my writing, she'll copy it. It's dead annoying.

In the conversation that followed, Poppy and Georgia both struggled to make sense of why Poppy's sister wanted to copy her, with Georgia asking 'Why? It's a bit silly', and Poppy concluding that 'She wants to annoy me.' Abigail, however, offered an explanation based on popular birth-order tropes: 'She wants to be like you. You're a role model', implying that Poppy's younger sister's wish to copy her, along with Poppy's own irritation about this, are an inevitable part of the normative expectations attached to their birth-order positions.

The idea of older siblings having the heightened responsibility of being a role model is pervasive. In a previous article (Davies, 2019) I explored how these feelings of responsibility are played out in the UK education system, where older siblings can feel a sense of responsibility to provide various types of social and academic support to younger siblings, even when relationships are not positive or the support is reluctantly given. The normative idea that older siblings ought to be role models and providers of care and support gives these relationships a particular 'stickiness' (Smart, 2007), making it difficult for young people to free themselves of their responsibility to their siblings in the context of school, even when siblings do not attend the same school at the same time. In the following focus group discussion, young people allude to these responsibilities of care and expand on some of the disadvantages of being a role model, which can manifest in 'getting the stick' (the blame) for younger siblings' misdemeanours:

Participant 1: [as the oldest sibling] You've *gotta* look after your brothers.

Participant 2: That you've gotta take care of them.

Interviewer: Right.

Participant 3: And sisters.

Interviewer: Okay.

Participant 4: And, and, erm, like they might not get the stick but you might get the stick for what they do.

Interviewer: Oh right. You do think, what, what sort of things? So if they're naughty or something?

Participant 4: Cos they'd say that they was trying to copy you.

Participant 2: Yeah.

Participant 3: Cos you're like their older sister.

Interviewer: Oh I see.

Participant: Or if they go and do summat wrong you *should* say, you *should* be setting an example or something like that.

[ages 14–15, St Stephen's, my emphases]

In this example we see the onus of care placed on older siblings through the emphasis on obligation in the repetition of '*you gotta* look after', '*you gotta* take care'. Young people also discuss the ways that parents reinforce the idea that older siblings ought to be a role model by expecting them to 'set an example', and by making them accountable for the behaviour of their younger brothers and sisters. Important here is the sense that older siblings *ought* to be a role model.

Interestingly, in their study of sibling relationships in Denmark, Ida Wentzel Winther and colleagues (2015a) point to an opposing normative idea that children ought not to feel burdened by their sibling relationships. They found that parents and daycare providers worked to ensure that sibling relationships were experienced as an emotional tie rather than one of care and responsibility. Indeed, normative rules about how siblings ought to be parented are also common, and there is a strong sense that siblings ought to be treated equally. Sue Heath (2018), in her study of the financial help given by parents to their grown-up children, found that young adults assumed that their parents would have divided resources fairly between them, even when they were not aware of the details of the help provided to their siblings. Of importance here are the ways in which normative rules about how siblingship ought to be done (including by parents) abound, despite the complex and contradictory nature of these relationships. For example, older siblings might find themselves acting as a role model for younger siblings and providing care for them while also feeling burdened and resentful of this obligation. Parents might find themselves striving to treat their children equally and to shield them from taking on too much responsibility, while also perpetuating birth-order-related roles and responsibilities through the expectation that older siblings might set an example. Though it appears that the burden of responsibility is often felt most keenly by older siblings, middle and younger siblings also have normative obligations attached to their birth-order positions, and young people in focus groups and interviews spoke of younger siblings being under pressure to be like their older siblings, with one young person saying 'it's like you *should* be more like them' (my emphasis).

In many ways it makes very little sense to think about birth-order roles in this way, as it is clear that they are diversely experienced and neither static nor easily defined (Wentzel Winther et al., 2015a). In her study of sibling groups of three, Samantha Punch found that lived experiences of birth order were negotiated, arguing that birth-order roles 'are not fixed hierarchies but can be subverted, contested, resisted and negotiated through children's everyday experiences of family life' (2008: 30). It is interesting though that, despite these nuances and diversities, normative understandings of birth-order roles pervade so strongly, particularly in childhood. It is also notable that there is often a gap between normative obligations and lived experiences.

In their study of familial obligation Finch and Mason (1993) argue that family obligations are negotiated in relation to particular lived relationships rather than fully prescribed by wider normative scripts, and found that generalised ideas (in response to a vignette) about moral obligation towards kin often did not map directly on to descriptions of actual practices (generated in qualitative interviews). This was because people's normative sense of obligation was combined in their lived relationships in negotiation with the context of that particular relationship (for example, the perceived quality of a particular tie). Thus normative imaginings of ideal sibling roles are practised in relation to the negotiated lived realities of relationships with siblings, even where there is discrepancy. In their study of the moral expectations associated with aunthood, Kinneret Lahad and Vanessa May (2021) similarly identify how aunts, as adult sisters, negotiate the ambiguous moral terrain of their role in relation to normative ideas about what they should do, as well as the personal histories of the relationships in which their role of aunt is embedded.

In his historical unpicking of the idealised 'family', John Gillis points out that '[h]umans have been imagining and reimagining family throughout recorded history' because, he proposes, our families are too fragile to satisfy what he terms 'the existential need for a sense of continuity, belonging and rootedness' (1997: xviii). Focusing on the symbolic dimensions of family, Gillis reveals the myth of the 'traditional' family, highlighting the growing importance of the symbolic families we live by. Gillis identifies 'a fundamental tension between the way families are and the way we would like them to be' (1997: xviii), what he terms the realities of the families we live with as opposed to the imagined and idealised families we live by.

In his book, Gillis outlines a number of relational forms and roles which are particularly imbued with this imagined idealism – including couples, mothers and fathers – where, although expectations about how these relationships ought to be lived have shifted over time, there remains a sense that traditional idealised relational forms are somehow lost. As Gillis writes, 'Never before had every father, mother and child been expected to be a role model' (1997: xix). I argue that siblings are a particularly profound example of the families we live by due to the strength of the norms and idealisation about sibling roles and responsibilities (including the expectation of being a role model), as well as the size of the gap between these and the realities of the siblings we live with. Gillis reminds us that, even though we might debunk the myths of our past traditional family values, this does not mean that we can stop living by these idealised family forms: 'We are no more able to live without our imagined families than were our ancestors' (1997: 18). According to Gillis, humans have always needed an imagined sense of family to provide a sense of 'continuity, belonging and rootedness' (1997: xviii) to overcome what he sees as the fragility of the realities of family life.

The following focus group discussion expresses these discrepancies between the families we live with and by. Here the young people – who are aged between 14 and 15 years old and from St Stephen's – are creating, 'live' in the focus group interaction itself, a set of moral and normative ideals about birth order and gendered sibling roles which are also troubled by their reflections on the realities of the sibling relationships in which they themselves are embedded. They are both working with and troubling tropes about the protective role of older, particularly male, siblings:

> Boy 1: Like I want a son about three years older than the girl cos then the boy can stick up for the girl if anything happens.
>
> Interviewer: Okay. So do you think, do you not think it can work the other way around then?
>
> Boy 1: Girls sticking up for lads?
>
> Participant: Not as much.
>
> Boy 2: It'd be better to have a sister that's like one year younger than you so you can keep an eye on her in school and that.
>
> …
>
> Participant: Yeah. But then you'll have all your time on them won't you?
>
> …
>
> Boy 2: So? You stick up for your relatives.
>
> Girl 1: But my brother never sticks up for me.
>
> Interviewer: Doesn't he?
>
> Girl 1: No. He'd just love me to get battered, he hates me.
>
> …
>
> Boy 2: So if someone were gonna come round to your house he'd do nowt. Even if it were a boy?
>
> Girl 1: No, he would batter a boy.
>
> Boy 2: Right then.
>
> [due to overlapping speech it has not been possible to identify individual voices]

This passage is indicative of the interplay between normative gendered roles about how older or younger, male or female siblings *ought* to behave towards each other, and descriptions of how their own sibling relationships work. The sense of moral 'rules' about how siblingship ought to be done is very strong here in what the boy is saying about family obligations; it does not matter that an older brother would have to spend time 'keeping an eye' on a younger sister because 'You stick up for your relatives.' The gender stereotyping also comes across strongly and resonates with Gillis's emphasis on the centrality of a sense of tradition in shaping the families we live by. What is interesting here is that these strong normative rules are challenged and resisted because they do not map on to the girl's own lived experience. This does not mean that normative ideals and lived relationships comprise 'made up' versus 'real' accounts of sibling roles, and we also learn from Gillis that we *need* the families we live by, however far removed from our day-to-day realities. In fact the different manifestations of siblingship presented in this interaction are mutually implicated and, along with the particularities of the research interaction itself, make up what Jaber F. Gubrium and James A. Holstein term the 'narrative environment'. Gubrium and Holstein explore the 'socially situated practice of storytelling (2009: 2), emphasising how narratives generated within qualitative interviews extend to other contexts 'in which stories were incited and told':

> Stories not only are told in interviews, but they also wend their way through the lives of story tellers. They are boundless in that regard, are told and retold, with no definitive beginning, middle or ends in principle, even while a sense of narrative wholes and narrative organisation is always in tow. (2009: 2)

In telling the stories of sibling relationships in this book, in particular in the previous chapter which focused more on narratives of the day-to-day realities of siblingship, young interview participants and mass observers are working with a collection of narratives about siblingship derived from their own experiences and observations, as well as from the ways sibling relationships are understood and represented in the wider cultural context. Thus, as Gubrium and Holstein argue in an earlier work, stories such as those about siblingship are 'reflexively linked to the *interplay* of discursive actions and the circumstances of storytelling' (1998: 164, original emphasis). Indeed, in the focus group example discussed above, we see the combination of lived experience and cultural norms in young people's accounts as they employ examples from their lived experiences with their siblings in order to help them to construct a narrative about the generalised moral implications of a particular birth-order position. We see this when the girl provides a contradictory reckoning of her older brother's role towards her in that she says he would not defend her, yet when confronted with a further moral scenario concerning a threat from a *boy* she concedes that her brother would provide protection. At the same time normative understandings are also drawn upon to help make sense of these lived relationships. Birth order and gender are very much present in narratives of the siblings we live by, even when they are less prescribed in our relationships with the siblings we live with and in our day-to-day sibling practices.

These ways in which normativity, morality, lived relationalities and imagination interweave in siblingship were particularly apparent in 14-year-old best friends Lyndsay and Gemma's very different ideas about being and having siblings. Lyndsay is one of six children. She has one older brother, one older sister, one younger brother and two younger sisters, ranging in age from 5 to 16, and she lives with her family in a three-bedroom house where she currently shares a room with her three sisters, having lived through many different bedroom-sharing configurations. Lyndsay described sharing a room with her siblings as incredibly difficult and has actively tried to find ways to gain more personal space, including a plan to move in with Gemma and another to move into the garden shed. Gemma, on the other hand, has lived most of her life as an only child, with her baby sister less than a year old at the time of the interview. In the following exchange the two friends are discussing why Gemma longs for an older sibling:

> Lyndsay: like when we were younger and I still had like a little brother in my room and she [Gemma] used to come round to mine and like it got dead hectic and stuff, so I don't think she would want any other brothers or sisters.

> Gemma: Well I do! I want an older brother or sister but too late now.

> Interviewer: Why do you think you would want an older brother or sister?

Gemma: Like to look up to and stuff.

...

Lyndsay: My older brother's a wuss! He doesn't do anything! Like and my big sister she's in a different school. And then my little brother, it's not as though he's gonna do anything.

The power of normative scripts in the shaping of imagined, idealised sibling configurations, particularly for children with no siblings, is clear in the way Gemma wishes for older siblings despite Lyndsay's first-hand experiences of the downsides of being from a large family. The reasons Gemma gave for wanting older siblings are highly reminiscent of the generalised moral norms of how older siblings are meant to behave (offering protection and being somebody to 'look up to') that were discussed in focus groups. Echoing the focus group conversation, Lyndsay also immediately counteracted these normative ideals with descriptions of the reality of her own sibling relationships, highlighting a gap between normative expectations and lived realities of birth order and siblingship which is, of course, classed, and here we see that Lyndsay's experience of being and having siblings is mediated by cramped living conditions.

It is clear that Gemma has observed the difficult realities of Lyndsay's sibling relationships and she even said to Lyndsay, 'You never stop arguing with your sister, every time I'm there you're always screaming at her.' However, even when faced with Lyndsay's increasingly persuasive descriptions of the difficulties of life with siblings, Gemma maintains her idealised normative imaginings:

Lyndsay: Like there's too, if there's like too many brothers and sisters like it'll get dead annoying because after a while you'll end up having loads of arguments that you're not speaking and stuff like that. And then you just don't like 'em. And then it causes trouble with the parents who's always arguing as well.

...

Gemma: They can look out for you, they can help you.

The strength of the discourse around older siblings providing help and protection suggests that it might be easier for Gemma, in her position as an almost 'only child', to draw on normative cultural discourses than on what she knows to be Lyndsay's more complex reality. Though the socio-economic position of Gemma's family is not clear, it is also possible that she experiences different material living conditions and is aware that, as such, her own experience of siblingship might be easier than Lyndsay's. Either way, Gemma is painting a picture of a different, ideal family scenario which it seems can live alongside her observations of her friend's family.

Even Lyndsay, with her observations of the difficulties of being and having siblings, imagines how life would be different if she occupied a different position in the sibship:

> Lyndsay: I wished I was the youngest.
>
> Gemma: Same cos then they can look out for you and stuff and you don't have a lot of worries.
>
> Lyndsay: And you get more attention.

Gemma and Lyndsay's discussion points to more than a reproduction of normative ideals of siblingship that survive in the face of the lived realities of being and having siblings. There is a yearning here for a life as a younger sister that never was, particularly in Gemma's account of it being 'too late now' for a big brother or sister. In the following section I explore this yearning in more detail, considering how tropes about siblingship are often drawn upon to conjure idealised imaginaries of what life would be like with that little sister to play with or big brother to look up to.

Yearned-for and imagined siblings

> It is easy to indulge a fantasy or daydream about what could have been. There is a certain satisfaction to be found in imagining a perfect and idyllic scene, poignantly heightened by our own exclusion from it. (Scott, 2019: 2)

Gemma and Lyndsay, along with the children in the focus group discussion above, are yearning for an imagined, idealised sibling relationship that never was. In progressing her 'sociology of nothing', Susie Scott explores the 'reverse biographical identity work' (2019: 1) that goes into imagining and accounting for things that have not been done, focusing on the ways people 'make sense of these no-things and no-bodies, folding them in to [their] life stories' (2019: 4).

Scott's sociology of nothing can help us to understand the meanings of sibling relationships through looking at what it means not to have siblings, or not to have a particular sibling relationship, for example with an older brother or sister.

Though having siblings is not a decision a person can make for themselves, their absence can be experienced as personal regret. As such, yearning for a sibling is reminiscent of Scott's 'invisible figures': 'ghostly, missing figures who seemed noticeably absent' (2019: 10) yet who could become an important part of people's biographical narratives. Scott's dataset of written stories includes the account of an adult woman, Imogen, who wrote about never having had siblings. Imogen writes: 'When I was growing up as an only child it always seemed that our family was incomplete and different from other "proper" families. I always felt that someone was missing and would have loved an older brother...' (quoted in Scott 2019: 16). Here Imogen is articulating her sense of absence at growing up without siblings. The reference to a lack of a 'proper' family is reminiscent of Gillis's (1997) families we live by, and following Gillis, we can understand that Imogen is perhaps yearning for a mythical idealised sense of what a 'family' ought to be as much as for an individual sibling. It is notable that Imogen specifies that she would have 'loved an older brother', echoing the idealised birth order and gendered sibling relationships and identities outlined by the young people in the focus group discussion in the previous section.

The narrative and imaginative work that Scott describes in the ways people construct alternative biographical narratives based on what could have been was something that Laura Towers (2020) also uncovered in her powerful sociological study of accounts of sibling bereavement. Many of Towers's participants, all of whom had experienced the death of a sibling as a child or young adult, reflected upon the sibling relationships that they had never had the chance to live. These imagined relationships were built upon common understandings of how sibling relationships might change through the life course, and as such, Towers's participants grieved an imagined closer adult sibling relationship where childhood conflicts might be resolved.

It is important to note that not everyone is able to perform this imaginative work. This lack of imaginative capability, for want of a better description, can occur when an existing sibling relationship is so deeply embedded in someone's life that an alternative reality cannot be conjured. In the following reflection, a 45-year-old male mass observer (B3227) is unable to reimagine a childhood without his brother, despite what he terms their 'fractious' relationship. He writes:

> Even though our relationship, when younger, was often fractious, I don't ever recall wishing that he did not exist. This seems, looking back, to have been unthinkable: not in the sense of being too shocking and unfraternal a notion to entertain, but of literally being beyond the limits of what I could conceptualize. My brother has always been a permanent fixture in my life and therefore his presence was not to be questioned or wished away.

It is telling that this man is simply unable to imagine an alternative siblingship because of the permanence of his relationship with his brother. This precisely echoes Carol Smart's (2007) explanation of the 'stickiness' of the relationships in which we are embedded, which I have previously applied to sibling relationships in the context of education (Davies, 2019).

Alongside the construction of alternative identities, Scott identifies a stigma attached to some of the absences described by her participants. In Imogen's case, the biographical identity of being an only child (an identity defined by an absence of siblings) is analysed by Scott as reminiscent of Erving Goffman's (1963) concept of stigma, in her identification of a societal assumption of only children as spoilt. Important here is Scott's identification of the role of others in labelling their non-self which supports an understanding of how stereotypes about not having siblings are experienced.

The following 80-year-old mass observer's account contains reflections of being, as she puts it, 'discriminated against' due to being an only child:

> I have no siblings. I always felt discriminated against by people who did not know me. They usually asked my name and if I had brothers or sisters. When I answered in the negative, the reply would be 'OK, so you're an *only* child' with a slight sneer. I had no advantages except excessive interest in me as a child and excessive responsibility in later life. I would have loved a brother or sister. I do think there are differences in your character depending on your position in the family hierarchy. The eldest child is usually more responsible, the middle

child more adventurous and the youngest more demanding but maybe I am prejudiced. Also these observations are generalised. [B22552, original emphasis]

The discrimination that this woman describes likely pertains to similar assumptions to those identified in Scott's research about how being an only child might affect someone's character. In this case the respondent takes care to debunk any ideas of being 'spoilt' in her description of the disadvantages she perceives herself to have experienced as a result of the absence of siblings. It is also notable that this respondent writes about her opinions about how birth order might affect a person's character. Despite her acknowledgement that she is generalising, the account the respondent gives of the characteristics attached to being an oldest, middle or youngest child speaks to the pervasiveness of these generalised stereotypes, even when, in the same account, the respondent is reflecting upon her own experiences of being at the receiving end of similar assumptions, which do not resemble her own perceptions. These experiences of being an only child were echoed in other mass observers' accounts, with one observer (B3227) recalling overhearing other adults talk about only children being spoilt, and suggesting that it was seen somehow as a selfish decision on the part of parents to only have one child.

The stereotyping described by some mass observers, along with Scott's respondent, Imogen, pertains to tropes about how children with no siblings turn out. The idea that only children are somehow spoilt is pervasive and can be found in many contexts, including China, where the one-child policy (which operated between 1979 and 2015) led to public concerns about the effect on a generation of citizens who were often dubbed spoilt 'little emperors' by the media (Connor, 2013). A number of psychologists also expressed concerns that children's personalities would be affected by the absence of siblings (see Liu et al., 2005). Interestingly, in her empirical study of the educational aspirations and achievements of adolescents born during the one-child policy, Vanessa Fong (2004) moved beyond the 'little emperors' stereotype to demonstrate the pressure young people were under due to unrealistically high expectations from parents. She also found that the dramatic change in childhood experiences caused generational tensions between adolescents and their parents. Fong usefully points to the sociological roots of the normative stereotypes concerning the effects of being a single child as well as the challenges of life as an only child: 'what mattered most was not their singleton status per se, but rather the fact that they were singletons in a society used to large families' (2004: 2).

Siblings and 'turning out': kinship expertise and lay understandings of relatedness

Idealised imaginings of yearned-for sibling relationships and the stereotypes held by others about those without siblings are tied up with assumptions about what our sibling roles mean for how we turn out in life. As outlined in the first chapter, public fascination with siblings often manifests in the application of lay persons' everyday kinship expertise to siblingship. Though there might not always be agreement as to how this works, there is a discursive sense that the accident of the configuration of a sibship will implicate how a person may turn out in life. We see this when people comment about being a typical oldest child, a 'daddy's little girl', through the commonly thought-of concept of 'middle child syndrome', and the ideas about being a self-contained or spoilt only child that were outlined above. Parenting books and online forums are filled with advice and threads about these topics. For example, there are many threads on the website Mumsnet, started mostly by mothers, worrying about so-called 'middle child syndrome'. Thread titles include 'Middle Child Syndrome...? Help!', 'Avoiding "Middle Child Syndrome"?!', 'What is your middle child like?' and 'Three of the same gender – middle child syndrome?' where contributors draw on their own experiences to advise a mother worried that if she had a third child, her middle child would become 'attention seeking' and 'awkward'. It is interesting that this risk is seen to be exacerbated by having three children of the same gender.

The idea that clues about a person's character, skills, education and so on can be found in their position in the sibship is not limited to lay person or public understandings, and many academic psychology studies of sibling relationships also seem to be based on the premise that one's birth-order position can determine aspects of how one might turn out in life. The pursuit of formulas pertaining to how sibship composition might affect people's outcomes in life seems somewhat outside the remit of sociological analysis because it does not explore the intersections of power structures such as class or race/ethnicity on sibling outcomes, and seems blind to the diversity and shifting complexities of family forms. However, psychological discourses such as those regarding siblingship have a strong effect on the ways people make sense of the self in contemporary society. In his analysis of the current regime of the self (introduced in Chapter 2), with its presumptions of a whole and complete identity or 'personality' waiting to be 'discovered' (1996: 39), Nikolas Rose traces this discursive self through the rise of the psy-sciences (psychology, psychiatry, psychoanalysis, psychotherapy and so on) which he describes as '"technologies of subjectification": the practical rationalities that human beings have applied to themselves and often in the name of self-discipline, self-mastery, beauty, grace, virtue, or happiness' (1996: 47). Rose argues that '[p]sychology constitutes its object in the process of knowing it' (1996: 49) and, with the help of 'experts', creates an ethic of the unique individual self. Thus psychological thinking and language become part of how we think about ourselves and our lives, and we find ourselves 'convinced that we should construe our lives in psychological terms of adjustment, fulfilment, good relationships, self-actualization and so-forth' (1996: 77). It is no surprise, then, that language and discourse from the psy-sciences have found their way into lived conceptualisations of siblingship and the way we make sense of how we turn out as siblings.

Many sociologists working in the fields of relationality and family life have argued strongly that morality, normativity and theoretical rules about how 'family' works derive from lived experience. See, for example, Finch and Mason (1993), who demonstrate how normative moral rules are negotiated within the lived realities of people's relationships; Jane Ribbens McCarthy, Ros Edwards and Val Gillies (2003), who demonstrate how the moralities of parenting in step-families are constructed; and of course David Morgan (1996), who argues that the very notion of 'family' resides in practices. This work notwithstanding, processes of abstracting, generalising and theorising are part of how people live and thus inform people's real-life relationships. We form theories and opinions about the world around us from various sources and these theories are part of our lives. Put simply, lay theories matter.

Andrew Sayer (2011) demonstrates the importance of 'lay normativity' for making sense of the social world, and Janet Carsten (2004: 4) calls for a focus on 'indigenous idioms' of kinship whereby lay understandings of how kinship works become the focus of academic analyses and theorisations of the meanings of relatedness. Indeed, anthropologists examining the kinship consequences of new reproductive technologies (NRTs) have pursued this through explorations of lay understandings of how these technologies might work in practice (Edwards, 2000; Franklin, 2003; Franklin and Mckinnon, 2001). In her ethnographic study of attitudes towards NRTs, kinship and community in the UK town of Bacup, Jeanette Edwards (2000: 204) talks about these lay understandings in terms of people having 'an expertise in kinship'. For Edwards, consideration of the ways that parents' values, characteristics, traits and so on can manifest in their offspring is ubiquitous, and is central to the sort of kinship thinking she terms 'Born and Bred thinking' (2000: 213). Born and Bred thinking centres around how things are passed on – from demeanour to genes and values. Edwards describes how her participants put their relationships with knowledge of others '*to work*' (2000: 207, my emphasis), using these specific lived experiences to reflect on more general and moral ideas about behaviours, actions and how things work. In figuring out how things work, Edwards argues that her participants mix elements that constitute kinship together in different ways depending on the situation:

> Not only are there inherited items passed on in 'the blood' or in 'the genes' and said to be given and immutable, but also characteristics imbued though example. There is not, however, a measurement of each in each person, but different elements of inheritance are congealed (purified) for different purposes. Different aspects of a person's make-up are made up (put together as in a prescription) according to the question being asked and the reasons for asking it. (2000: 216)

In the following focus group example (of 13–14-year-olds at Highfields), young people discuss the 'rules', as they see them, which govern how siblings turn out. There is a great deal of disagreement here, but participants are thinking through how the accident of birth order might affect them, and in doing so are drawing upon their own expertise. The lively nature of the exchange is also indicative of the level of interest in the discussion and supports arguments made by both Mason and Tipper (2008) and Hayley Davies (2015) that children employ kinship expertise and engage with lay theorising about how kinship works:

Joanna: Usually younger siblings do worse.

Haashim: Wiser, are wiser.

Interviewer: Why do you think that?

Joanna: No, it's just like been proved in tests because parents like wrap their first child in bubble, like bubble wrap and do like everything for them and that and then the second child is...

...

Interviewer: So does anyone agree with that view that younger siblings...?

Haashim: A bit.

Participant: No.

Interviewer: Why, so you say a bit, why do you think a bit? [overlapping]

Emma: They don't like

Haashim: [overlapping] The older guy getting more attention. However the, the younger guy's wiser.

Participant: Younger siblings [inaudible] like if you do mess up.

Zac: I think, well it's in my family ... My brother's told me not to mess about in school cos it's getting to the most important time

...

Emma: Well in my family it's like, erm, well my parents were kind of like experimenting in how to bring my sister up and then so she got away with more stuff. And then they learned to trust her more so she does better like on her own. But with me they've kind of like wrapped me in bubble wrap rather than the first person, their first child. [laughs]

Haashim: Learned from their mistake. [overlapping]

Interviewer: [laughs] What do other people think do they, does anybody else think it might have something to do with whether you're the youngest or the oldest?

Haashim: Well I don't know.

Interviewer: No you don't why, why's that?

Zoe: Cos I'm the youngest and I'm the rebel

In discussing the rules about how siblings turn out, participants in this focus group are drawing on their kinship expertise, applying their own experiences and observations of their relationships. This expertise sits alongside normative ideas about, for example, the ways parents treat siblings and the effects of this parenting on children (wrapping the oldest child in 'bubble wrap', for example). Young participants are also drawing upon generalised ideas about scientific evidence, and it is telling that Joanna states that it has been 'proven in tests', alluding to the importance of psy-'expert' knowledge in the ways she makes sense of how siblingship works to create the unique discoverable self (Rose, 1996), even though this idea of 'proof' remains a rather abstract idea. This discussion also includes different types of thinking/theorising about siblingship in ways similar to Edwards's (2000) observation that various modes of 'passing on' are drawn upon in different combinations for a multitude of purposes. For example, claims about the significance of differences in parenting styles for different birth-order positions exist alongside references to so-called 'tests' which 'prove' the theories put forward about the salience of birth-order position. There is also a challenge from Emma, who utilises the same frames discussed earlier in the group (the concept of being 'wrapped in bubble wrap') to narrate her own experience, troubling the theory being produced collectively that it is older siblings whom parents overprotect.

Although participants in this focus group could not identify a universal rule linking temperament and parenting styles to particular birth-order positions, it is clear that participants understood parents to be fallible, regularly making mistakes and learning from these, and that these parenting practices contribute to how siblings turn out according to their birth-order position. Young people's expertise in these discussions was derived from a combination of normative tropes about birth order and their own lived experiences of their family relationships. Similarly to Emma in the example above, in the following example from a focus group discussion, 14-year-old Shelley from Highfields used the general premise of birth-order-specific parenting styles to think about the complexities of her own experiences of being parented alongside her siblings. Here Shelley highlights the idea that parents are learning and adapting their practices as they go along, and she suggests that her mother parented her differently from her older brother after learning from the mistakes she made with him:

> I think it's like, you know like my mum? Like I've got an older brother and he's left school but she weren't so much on his case about being good, so when *he* left, and she thought that, you know, cos he's not done anything with his life, he's just at home and that, she wants me to be an example for my little sister. So she's more on my case than what she was with him, so, we were quite, one child to leave school and she knows that he, she wants the other child to become like…

Mass observers also commonly referred to rules about birth order and how siblings might turn out in life. The following 54-year-old woman (G3042), who has one older brother and one younger sister, appears very much to identify as a 'middle child'. Though she does not state what characteristics a middle child might possess or why, she claims to be able to recognise something of middle-childness in herself and others: 'I believe the psychology of it. You can tell when you met someone, often, what their family position has been/is. Sometimes I end up speaking with "middle children" at parties and we both recognise it.' It is interesting that this mass observer talks about believing the 'psychology of it'. Here psychology seems to be drawn upon less as scientific evidence provided by experts, such as Joanna's tests that 'prove' her theories about parenting and birth order, and more as something magical or spiritual that requires faith or belief.

As outlined in the introduction, siblings are often used as a kind of living 'test case' for thinking about the role of nature and nurture in how people turn out. Take tennis champion sisters Venus and Serena Williams and the questions we might ask about them and where their extraordinary talent came from, questions which weigh up the conundrum of how parenting, opportunity and practice mix with genetic inheritance to produce talent. When considering similarities between siblings, it is common to draw on the idea of something being 'in the genes' as a sort of shorthand for the mysteries of family resemblances and of 'passing on'. In her discussion of 'ineffable kinship' outlined in the previous chapter, Jennifer Mason observes that, although people often refer to 'genes' or 'nature/nurture', they often don't seem to mean, '"genetics" as defined by scientists' (2018: 88). Mason goes on:

> Instead, they used these terms when they were struggling to capture in words and to explain the mysterious potency of a life force that formed such a routine yet magical part of their everyday experience of relatedness. 'Genetics' and 'nature', in that sense were both shorthand and metaphor for something altogether more experimental, ethereal and sensory than any scientific concepts. (2018: 88)

We saw some of these mysteries about the connection between siblings in the discussion of resemblances in the previous chapter. Here we see the idea of 'genes' being used when people are trying to work out the rules relating to why siblings might be similar or different.

Take the following extracts from focus group discussions in which young people are discussing where talents come from. In these examples participants are talking excitedly over the top of one another and it is not possible to ascertain who is speaking:

[It comes from] Genetics.

...

Genes.

No.

Interviewer: Why do you disagree?

Cos it's like some mums can be different.

[overlapping] No, it's just the upbringing.

Like ... David Beckham he likes football or Rooney or somebody, they didn't get it from their mum or dad did they?

No but it gets passed down generations.

They've got a *natural* talent.

How does it?

You're telling me...

We'd all be the same then cos we all came from the same two people didn't we?

[overlapping] Yeah, Adam and Eve.

[overlapping – shouting to be heard] You *work* on it.

It could just be upbringing ... Like if you live in the house and like someone goes, say, does art and then, cos my mum does art and that's why I do it...

[overlapping] ... play football since the day you were born you'd be good at it aren't you? ... Like if I had a son and I sent him boxing when he was young he'd be good when he gets older cos he's done it for so long.

Natural.

(ages 14–15, St Stephen's, my emphases)

[discussing what can be 'in your genes']

Talents.

Sport.

Knowledge.

Interviewer: So say, you said sport talent can be in the genes? So do you think that some people are born more sporty than others?

Yeah.

Yeah.

How do you be born well sporty?

It can be like doing lots of sports.

Running.

No cos your parents can be like dead active and fit and then when you're born some of that can be passed on can't it? Like health.

Through the genes.

Healthy babies.

(ages 11–12, St Stephen's)

In these examples, young people are basically discussing 'nature' and 'nurture', though they are not framing it that way. They are drawing on a range of knowledge and experience to figure out where talents come from. The use of 'genes' or 'genetics' seems to stand for a general sense of a sort of fixed inheritance. In the second example, when pushed to think about the implications of genetics (that some people might be born 'more sporty' than others), participants began to question the simplicity of it being 'in the genes' before ultimately referring to the use of the concept as a catch-all trope when the questions about multiple modes of transmission posed by the participant towards the end of the conversation became too complex. The phrase 'healthy babies' is interesting here, as a discursive idea that can be used to explain nature and nurture.

In addition to 'genetic thinking', thinking through how siblings turn out, particularly when they turn out differently, can encourage a particularly sociological reflexivity in considering the role of the 'nurturing environment'. In a focus group discussion, for example, Farhana made the comment, 'We [her and her sisters] all seem to be like in the same bubble', with the metaphor of a shared 'bubble' conjuring images of shared upbringing akin to ideas of habitus. Britney (in an interview at the holiday club) articulated a similar view when she discussed how members of a family have 'similar surroundings'. Of course, siblings often do turn out differently (Conley, 2004), and even when siblings have grown up in the same household and have attended the same school, they experience their family, school and wider society differently. In this way their environment can never be identical, and in the following chapter I look more closely at the role of timing in shaping the way siblingship is done.

Both Edwards and Mason describe a mixing or tangling of different factors that are brought into play when people are trying to work out how things are 'passed on' (Edwards, 2000) or solve the mysteries of 'ineffable kinship' (Mason, 2018). This tangling comes through clearly in the following example, in which 14-year-old cousins Joseph and Britney are discussing Joseph's little brother Anis:

Joseph: [talking about his younger brother Anis] He looks like I was when I was younger.

Interviewer: Really?

Joseph: Yeah.

Interviewer: Yeah? And do you think that that means that when he grows up he's likely to be similar to you in other ways as well?

Joseph: Similar, yes. Not, he's not gonna look like me though.

Interviewer: Do you... Why, why not do you think?

Joseph: Cos it's, erm, proven because we're gonna eat different things and our faces are gonna grow in different ways because of the stuff we eat and, erm, I, he's gonna probably eat a lot healthier than me, so...

...

Britney: I'm similar to my brother.

...

Interviewer: In what way do you think you're similar to your brother?

Britney: Like, like, looks because we've both got, like, the same parents, but my sister, she's, like, my half-sister cos she's got a different dad. And it's my mum that's, that's in us all that you can see that we're related. Erm, but with me and Lewis, it's, like, our parents cos you can see, see it in us both and, like, like, erm, the face, like, it's, it's round and so is my little brother's and they're, like, the hair colour, and then eye colour sometimes.

In this discussion of resemblances we see a combination of different ideas that Joseph and Britney draw upon when thinking about how Anis might turn out. The evidential nature of resemblances discussed in the previous chapter comes across clearly in Britney's discussion of how her mother is 'in us all', and that it is possible to work out the complexities of her blended family through visual observation. What is important here is the different tropes and ideas that come together to form a sense of how siblings turn out. Joseph, for example, draws on a pseudo-scientific idea of 'proof' and also points to the interactions of given or inherited characteristics and environmental factors (including diet and nutrition, which Joseph is likely to have studied at school) in determining how his brother will look when he is older. Though the combination of factors that are drawn upon to work out what makes up a person's characteristics vary, there is a common sense that some sort of rules apply, that these can somehow be 'proven', and that these questions become concentrated when applied to sibling relationships, where a comparison of similarities and differences between siblings can seem to unlock some of the complexities of the nature versus nurture conundrum.

Conclusion

This chapter has shifted the focus from the lived experiences of being a sibling and having sibling relationships to consider the ways we imagine siblings and siblingship to be. In so doing I have explored understandings of what siblings ought to be, how they might be conjured or idealised in our imaginary worlds, and how we draw upon other discursive ideas about nature and nurture to make sense of how siblingship works, with siblings providing a tool or lens for thinking through the mysteries of kinship and how things are passed on in families.

It is clear that imagination is an important facet of siblingship. Though this chapter has pointed to a gap between normative imaginings of what a sibling ought to be and the lived complexities of siblingship that I discussed in the previous chapter, these imagined siblings are no less real and interact with our practices of doing siblingship. The siblings we live by inform the siblings we live with and vice versa. This gap between normative understandings and lived experiences has been identified by other authors (Finch and Mason, 1993; Gillis, 1997), but the particularities of sibling relationships, in terms of both the ambivalences and complexities that characterise these relationships (outlined in the previous chapter) as well as the interaction of multiple discursive and normative frames about roles and responsibilities, ideal siblings and 'nature' versus 'nurture', means that siblings can be a fruitful way of sociologically exploring interactions between normative ideas and personal relationships. The background nature of 'being there' among siblings, along with the ups and downs of many sibling relationships, means that the gap between expectations and imaginings of siblingship and the lived realities of being and having siblings can be large. Thus siblings can be particularly revealing of the complexities of how normative ideas are negotiated.

Indeed, by thinking with siblings, sociologists are encouraged to extend their understandings of people's imaginary worlds beyond the idea of normativity. In looking at siblings we have seen how the idealised siblings we live by (Gillis, 1997) create imagined or yearned-for siblings, which implicate the ways people might see themselves and their lives 'turning out'. Normative ideas of sibling relationships also interact with lay understandings of how kinship works and how things are passed on, which creates a sense of how different configurations of sibling relationship ought to turn out. The weaving together of these less explored facets of the imaginary help direct the sociological gaze beyond discourse to consider how these ideas actually manifest in and affect people's lives, relationships and sense of self.

Chapter 5

Time

Temporality implicates all aspects of siblingship. Themes raised in the previous chapters such as closeness, care, identity, resemblance and normative scripts about how siblings ought to behave towards one another all pertain to temporality in some way. Sibling relationships change and evolve as we progress through the life course, as the significance to who we are and how we live of being one in a series of siblings waxes and wanes as we age and experience various life events. Biological age, birth order and age gap shape the lived experiences of siblingship as well as the ways in which we imagine brothering and sistering ought to be done. From the everyday knowledge gleaned through growing up together in the same home to 'special' moments in family time and the generational proximity that accompanies sharing similar life course transitions at similar times, different facets of temporality profoundly affect siblingship.

This chapter will explore the ways sibling relationships shift, evolve, ebb and flow through the life course, attending to how siblings may become closer as they grow older or drift apart as they age. This evolution of the sibling relationship over time is moulded by critical moments in the life course such as progressing through the education system, having children, redundancy, divorce, bereavement, illness and so on. Alongside these pivotal moments, the chapter will consider the role of the temporal rhythms of everyday family life in the ways siblingship is done, from the embodied proximity and enhanced 'knowing' that comes from growing up in the same home as children to the role of certain family traditions or occasions such as Christmas, Eid, birthdays and family holidays which have their own temporal qualities. In her study of sistering, Melanie

Mauthner (2005b) conceptualises changes in sistering over time in terms of external factors, such as life events like motherhood, marriage, divorce and death, and internal factors, such as shifting power relationships and changing subjectivities. This chapter will explore the ways these internal and external changes are tangled together in sibling relationships.

Following George Herbert Mead's (1980 [1932]) analysis of clock or calendar time as a social convention that can never exist independently of an individual's perspective, we can understand age gap and birth order as social constructs that may be experienced differently in different relationships and at different times. As such, it is possible to trace how they can shift and evolve over time and in different contexts. Samantha Punch (2005) has shown how, rather than being fixed by biological age, birth order is negotiated, challenged and undermined in the relationships of siblings whose generational proximity means they share a 'backstage' relationship, less characterised by age-related hierarchies than relationships with parents. Furthermore, the generational proximity of many siblings can also mean that, rather than the individualised routes to adulthood described by Ulrich Beck (1992) in his thesis on the 'risk society', older siblings can provide a 'route map' to adulthood as they navigate similar education systems, job and housing markets a few years before their younger brothers or sisters. However, even relatively small age gaps can become significant, as siblings may experience different socio-economic eras and be affected by shifts in public policy (such as changes in university tuition fees or benefits systems) in different ways. The chapter will also touch upon the ways siblings might experience different eras in family time and how these differences can challenge the gold standard of equality highlighted in the previous chapter as the lynchpin of the 'good' parenting of siblings.

This chapter explores these temporalities of siblingship, unravelling some of the nuances of time in relation to siblings and pointing to the importance of a temporal understanding of siblingship. In so doing, themes raised earlier in the book are revisited in order to focus particularly on their temporal qualities, and new themes are introduced. A temporal analysis of siblings is particularly illuminating – inviting the linking of age, generation, life course, everyday life, family time, critical moments and the serendipitous idea of being in the wrong place in the life course at the wrong time in history in ways that can illuminate the interconnection of these temporalities.

Narrating siblingship through a temporal lens

I begin this chapter with a discussion of one mass observer's account of her sibling relationships. G4466 is a woman in her forties. She had a younger brother who died as a baby when the writer was around three years old, and has a sister who is five years younger and whom she describes with a long list of adjectives about her character ('big-hearted', 'dependable', 'stroppy'), talents ('artistic', 'gardener', 'whistler', 'great cook') and their relationship ('important', 'loved', 'dismissive', 'supportive'). Over the next seven pages of her response to the directive on siblings, the mass observer describes her relationship with her sister, reflecting on how it has changed over time, the role of ageing in the shaping of their relationship and the significance of childhood memories. The story is punctuated by several pivotal events which impact upon the nature of the relationship. Past, present and future are woven together in the telling of the story of the sisters, with their relationship narrated through a temporal lens. By opening the discussions in this chapter with an in-depth analysis of the role of time in this mass observer's account, I demonstrate how different facets of temporality interact in the ways siblingship is lived and imagined, and show how key themes raised in previous chapters, such as resemblance, identity, contact and care, are temporally situated.

The mass observer described her changing relationship with her sister, who as a baby was 'the best doll anyone could have had', but with whom the relationship went 'downhill all the way after she became a toddler'. Childhood memories are evoked to explain the difficulties of their relationship as children. These memories are centred on material and embodied elements such as clothing and their relationship to their growing bodies and age: 'I have very fond memories of white smocks with tiny little red flowers on them and jeans – I was outrageously jealous when I grew out of mine and it was handed down to her'; toys also feature, as the writer describes the personal politics over who got the blonde and brunette Sindy dolls, which she still has as an adult. Memories of particular arguments are also relayed: 'I once wound her up so much that she took her shoe off and hit me in the eye with the heel of it and gave me the only black eye I've ever had in my life.'

The four- to five-year age difference between the sisters was cited as a cause of some of the tensions between them as children, and, though her parents were 'fair' and 'even handed', the writer notes that her younger sister was allowed to do things sooner, such as having piano and dance lessons, and the observer was often expected to look after her. This was connected to the changing economic position of the family, and the observer was aware that her sister had benefited from financially easier times, with their parents able to buy her the piano lessons that they could not afford when the respondent wanted them.

The mass observer identifies a particular moment when her sister was around 14 or 15 that she describes as a 'significant shift' in their relationship. The observer threw a 1920s style cocktail party when their parents were away, and allowed her sister to come with some of her friends:

> She suddenly shifted to being part of my world, able to contribute and participate on the same level and not be five years my junior stuffing up my fun. She got outrageously drunk and puked down the back door steps, shut the door and carried on partying – class!

Following the party, the observer describes having that 'mate/sister thing now', and this reduction in the significance of their age gap seems to have characterised their relationship into adulthood. The writer goes on to describe how her relationship with her sister continued to evolve in adulthood, weathering other pivotal moments such as a joint holiday when relationships were strained. Even physical resemblances between the sisters have evolved over time: 'She's taller and currently bigger – in the past I've been bigger.'

Despite a general sense of a relationship that has improved over time, the mass observer expresses feelings of anxiety about the future of her relationship with her sister. Writing as she was about to embark on a return to university study, the observer wonders how her changed financial circumstances while she funds her studies, along with her sister's seeming lack of interest in her academic endeavours, will affect their relationship. In light of her reflection that she might no longer be able to afford to go and stay with her sister, who lives some distance away, the observer notes the importance of everyday knowledge for relationships, writing that 'To be close you need to know someone's trivia, day to day nonsense. When that goes then what is left is a sort of acquaintanceship.' In narrating the story of her relationship with her sister, the respondent also looks further into the future, predicting how things might change again as a result of these growing differences in their financial situations as well as contemplating caring for their parents in their old age. Both sisters had to care for their grandmother in their teens and this has deterred them from taking on other caring roles, including having children. The observer wonders about the consequences of one parent surviving the other, predicting, 'if it's Dad it will be a breeze, he'll sort himself out but Mum expects to live with one of us – we neither of us consider this viable … We don't do "care". We will have a hell of a time when the time comes.'

This account of a sibling relationship illuminates important temporal themes. We see the way the relationship evolves over time, from the younger sibling being a little 'doll', to an annoying child, to a 'mate', and then the gaze is taken further into the future as the observer wonders whether the relationship will become less 'mate-like' and more of an acquaintanceship as her circumstances change. In doing this thinking, the writer spans past, present and future, evoking childhood memories of objects and events, identifying pivotal or seminal moments that signify a shift in the ways her relationship with her sister was lived, practised and understood in the past, and predicting future such moments. The observer also points to the role of family 'eras', such as changes in the family's financial position, identifying how they affected the sisters differently. We see how the role of age shifts over time, and the 1920s party represents a kind of 'coming of age' moment in their lives, as her little sister marked her rite of passage into 'mate' territory by participating in adult activities (getting drunk) and demonstrating her competence in this (she carried on partying after she had vomited on the step).

I now move on to unpack some of these temporal themes, considering how temporality affects sibling relationships as well as reflecting on how a focus on siblingship can push some of our sociological understandings of time in different directions.

Temporal convoys and being there through the life course

Given that they can be among our most long-lasting relationships, we often make our way through the life course as a sibling. In Chapter 3, following Julie Brownlie's work on 'ordinary' relationships (2014), I discussed how care between siblings is not always overtly exchanged but can instead take the form of 'being there'. This being there among siblings can have longevity, and siblings may provide this background support through the life course. This long-term 'there-ness' resonates with John Gillis's concept of temporal convoys. Gillis explains: '[the] convoy metaphor summons up an image of safety from the dangers lurking just below the surface, and indeed, temporal convoys offer us reassurance against the ravages of time and the fact of human finitude' (1997: 43).

The idea of a temporal convoy as a source of comfort and reassurance over time resonates with the temporal qualities of being there as a reliable long-term presence. Of course, not all sibling relationships are positive sources of comfort and reassurance, and Carol Smart's work on embeddedness and the 'sticky' nature of some relationships that are difficult to 'shake free from … at an emotional level' (2007: 45) helps us to understand how relationships can continue to influence our thoughts and practices even when experienced as negative or destructive.

The significance of travelling through life alongside one's siblings and being there through time came across in many mass observers' reflections. D996 – an 85-year-old woman – is an only child who decided to write about the relationship between her two grand-daughters, aged 29 and 25. She described how they did not get along very well when they were young and had very different aspirations for their futures, living in different countries and rarely seeing one another. However, she observed how the sisters were a key source of support for one another when their parents separated. The way their grandmother describes their relationship is reminiscent of Gillis's 'temporal convoys' as she alludes to the role of the sibling relationship as an anchor point during the various trials and tribulations of adult life. She writes: 'They are very much constants in each other's lives when all around them is changing in terms of careers and boyfriends.' Of course, it is significant that we do not have the perspectives of the sisters themselves here, and it may be the case that, as an only child herself, this mass observer is imagining an idealised sibling relationship in her observations of her grandchildren akin to the normative ideals of how a sibling relationship ought to look explored in the previous chapter. Regardless of the possible interactions between lived experience and imagined ideals, the idea of a sibling as a temporal convoy resonates strongly in this account.

Another feature of the longevity of sibling relationships that came across in the mass observer's experiences used to introduce this chapter is the changing nature of siblingship across the life course. C4988 – a 58-year-old man with one older sister and one older brother – described in his response to the Mass Observation directive how his relationship with his siblings has changed. His sister, who is ten years older, tried to 'mother' him as a child, and he recalled regular arguments with his brother which were exacerbated by cramped living conditions. Despite these hardships, the respondent describes how this bond has continued through the life course and reflects that he now gets along better with his siblings and that, although contact has at times been less frequent, it increased again following the death of their father. It is in their shared childhood experiences of growing up poor that the respondent sees the 'bond' between himself and his siblings being formed. This bond formed through childhood adversity was activated at important and difficult moments, and the observer reflects on how much more difficult the recent illness and death of his mother would have been without his siblings, who he describes as supporting one another by sharing the practical arrangements.

Even young people who took part in interviews about their sibling relationships recalled how their own sibling relationships had changed over time. In the example below, friends Lois and Molly (both white British, aged 14 and interviewed together at the estate youth club), reflect on how their relationship with their siblings has improved as they have entered later childhood:

> Lois: I always used to always argue with them, all of my brothers, and then when we reached our, like, older ages, we all, we just sat down in the living room and said, 'Look, it's no point arguing about now, we might as well all just be closer than like we was when we were all little.'
>
> Molly: That's the same for me!

Lois: Now we just tell each other everything, so, any problems we just sit down and talk about it, and then it all just gets sorted out from there, so.

Mass observer E4825 – an 18-year-old woman – similarly reflects on how she has become closer to her 15-year-old brother as they have become teenagers, commenting on how they stick together if one is arguing with their parents, and noting that she thinks they have become more alike as they have aged. She also anticipates how their relationship might evolve in the future, commenting that she expects that they will exchange more forms of assistance, including financial, when they reach an age when their parents are no longer their primary source of support. G3963 – a 40-year-old female mass observer with three younger siblings (a brother and two half-siblings) – reflected that despite the advantages of having someone to play with in childhood, the reason sibling relationships tend to improve in adulthood is that, as with other things in life, you have to 'grow up' in order to appreciate your siblings.

So we can see that sibling relationships change through the life course. Here we have seen examples of mainly positive change as siblings move on from the arguments and physical fighting that characterise many sibling relationships in childhood. However, as touched upon in Chapter 3, some mass observers spoke of a decline in closeness due to geographical distance or partnering. The mass observer discussed at the beginning of this chapter also predicted a future decline in her sibling relationship when she envisioned that her financial situation would make visiting more difficult. In the same way that improvements to the quality of the sibling relationship were caused by moving out of childhood into adult relationships, declines in sibling relationships are also often caused by life course shifts. Cameron, a 13-year-old boy interviewed in his school, talked about how, despite not having what he calls a 'typical' sibling relationship in childhood – where older siblings ignore their younger brothers and sisters – his relationship with his middle brother changed once he got a girlfriend:

No, we all get along, we're not like your typical older brother when you see 'em all like always in the room and not talking to you and stuff. We're not like that because we're all a pretty close family but … My middle brother he's with his girlfriend a lot now so he's, I don't see him that much. But when I do see him … But I mean I see him quite a lot but I don't see him as much, he puts his girlfriend first now so he's just … Like before then, you, I saw him all the time but now he's put his girlfriend first I don't see him that much. But my older brother who also has his girlfriend but he doesn't, he's not like that, he'll … Like my middle brother he's protective of her…

Here the sibling relationship has changed as his brother has reached a new stage in his life – getting a girlfriend – and the priorities and patterns of his relationships have shifted.

A number of mass observers wrote about how their different life experiences left them with less in common with their siblings as they aged. In Chapter 2 I explored the seriality of siblingship and the effect of this on people's sense of self and identity. The comparability of siblings is heightened during childhood, and can lessen as people's lives are shaped by different experiences and they become less readily compared, particularly by actors beyond the family such as teachers and others in the locality. As the influences on their lives become increasingly diverse, siblings also become a less satisfying case study for pondering questions of nature versus nurture. However, a number of mass observers were still able to look back and compare the different life choices and experiences of themselves and their siblings, observing the effects of these differences. One 46-year-old male mass observer (E5014) commented that physical resemblances between him and his brother have diminished as they have aged, and that they look less alike now than they did when they were in their twenties and thirties. He puts this down to their different lifestyles, with his brother working outdoors in a physical job and him working in an office as a civil servant:

While my brother used to be naturally much slimmer than I, he now does very little exercise, no sport, smokes occasionally, and doesn't eat a particularly healthy diet. Consequently, despite being three years younger than me I'm sad to see he looks older, and he's suffered from a few health problems such as blood pressure.

The idea that siblings will 'be there' at key life course moments is a powerful one that can exist even in relationships that have drifted or become less close over time. In line with Finch and Mason's (1993) account of how family responsibilities are negotiated, wider normative ideas about the support that siblings ought to provide one another are negotiated within the lived realities of the sibling relationship and its changing qualities. In addition to siblings coming together to deal with the illness or death of their parents, mass observers also reported supporting their siblings through difficult life events such as illness and divorce. E5040 is a 48-year-old man. He has one sister who is just over a year younger than him. His sister was living with a terminal cancer diagnosis at the time of writing, and the observer commented, 'it is highly unlikely that we will grow old together, which is a very strange feeling'. The observer described how his and his sister's lives had taken different paths over the years, despite their being playmates and having similar childhood experiences due to their close ages. Though they have always visited one another they have been in much more regular contact since his sister's illness.

We have seen that sibling relationships ebb and flow through the life course, coming into sharp relief at certain critical moments and sometimes drifting at others. As opposed to Anthony Giddens's individualised and reflexive 'fateful moments', defined as 'times when events come together in such a way that an individual stands at a crossroads in their existence or where a person learns of information with fateful consequences' (1991: 113), these moments are embedded in relationships, shaped by shared memories and biographies. Shared past experiences are an important facet of being there, and in the examples above we have seen the ways the past is evoked in how people make sense of the shifts in their sibling relationships. According to Brownlie:

> The way that shared experience of particular episodes or lives – in the absence of talk – comes to deepen a sense of others being 'on our side'. This privileged knowledge ... involves a sense of someone else *understanding* our feelings or experiences, based on knowledge of what we're going through and/or us as individuals. Over time, this insider knowledge and experience of 'thereness' is jointly lived and sedimented ... Being 'there' in the present often involves, then, having been there in the past. (Brownlie 2014: 135, original emphasis)

This sort of privileged knowledge, formed through shared childhood experiences, can be felt particularly strongly by siblings who know the details of one another's upbringing in ways others cannot share. For many people, no one understands their parents from quite the same vantage point as them, and their sibling(s) often know one another in ways that others who may come to take on a more 'important' role in adulthood, such as partners, friends or children, can never share. Indeed, in her discussion Brownlie goes on to provide an example of a participant whose brother understood her grief following the death of their parents: 'Coz he's ma brother. Because he knew, didn't he? [...] He knew that. We were both going through the same things' (2014: 136). The death of parents is a pivotal moment for many siblings not only as a point when they may come together to offer emotional and/or practical support, but also because the temporalities of a shared upbringing can produce enhanced mutual understandings unique to siblings, and many mass observers commented on being grateful for their siblings at this time. Of course, these moments can also signify a lack of support, and normative expectations around sharing responsibilities for a sick parent or handling funeral arrangements together with a sibling can mean a lack of support at times like these is keenly felt.

In her analysis of Mass Observation accounts of belonging across the lifetime, Vanessa May points to the ways in which time itself can be an important source of belonging, contributing to 'a sense of ease with yourself and surroundings' (2018: 306). May points to the importance of people's past and future in the cyclical ways they make sense of and narrate their lives, preferring the term 'lifetime' to 'life course' to avoid reducing her analysis of time to life-stages and countering assumptions about old age as a time of reminiscence. Some of the ways in which sibling relationships are temporally situated seem particularly important to their feelings of belonging in time, with siblings often sharing memories of the past and anticipating future moments of closeness and distance as well as perhaps situating themselves in time alongside their sibling 'temporal convoys'.

Generational proximity and relational transitions

May's call to move beyond the life course in analysing personal experiences of temporalities notwithstanding, the generationally proximate nature of many sibling relationships means that being and having a sibling can profoundly affect key life course events or transitions, because siblings often experience age-related institutions (such as school) as well as socio-economic and familial contexts at similar times. Karl Mannheim distinguishes between 'concrete social groups' such as families, where members have a knowledge of one another and a sense of forming a group, and 'generations' which are 'mere collective facts' (1952: 288):

> Generation location is based on the existence of biological rhythm in human existence – the factors of life and death, a limited span of life, and ageing. Individuals who belong to the same generation, who share the same year of birth, are endowed, to that extent, with a common location in the historical dimension of the social process.
> (Mannheim, 1952: 290)

Siblings often share a generation in the sense that they occupy a common sociohistorical location, even if they do not share the same year of birth, as well as sharing a 'concrete group' in the form of the family they grew up in, where in turn they experience shared micro socio-economic eras of the family. Of course this is not always the case, and even where siblings are close in biological age, the macro and micro eras they inhabit can be quite different (we saw this in the mass observer's account of not being able to afford piano lessons discussed in the opening sections of this chapter). In the previous chapter I pointed to the importance of fairness and equality between siblings, particularly in terms of the ways they are parented. Shifts in the eras of family time (Mason and Muir, 2013) can mean that siblings find themselves growing up with different levels of financial resources, in different houses or areas. Christopher Ince, Anne Chappell and Ellen McHugh's (2021) study of students raised in military families demonstrated how children of different ages were affected differently by their families' constant moving, with siblings experiencing varying effects of starting new schools at different points in their education.

Furthermore, macro socio-economic shifts can mean that siblings who might be very close in age can face vastly different financial or cultural circumstances, with public policy and other changes creating cleavages between the life chances of siblings. In the UK, for example, the introduction of large tuition fees for university education in 2012–13 left many siblings in very different financial positions. Similarly, the 2007 global economic crisis and subsequent austerity politics implemented in many countries left some siblings facing very different housing and job markets. Sue Heath (2018) pointed to the role of UK families in the support parents provided to their children in purchasing their home, with many young people in the study feeling sure that their parents would have accounted for shifts in the housing market among other factors when working out how to equally support their children. Finch and Mason in their study of wills and inheritance also found that parents often tried to ensure *'equality of outcome'* (2000: 53, original emphasis) when bequeathing money or property to their children, accounting for different contexts and circumstances in order to make things fair. More recently, the COVID-19 pandemic has affected children of different ages differently; as outlined in the opening passage of this book, in the UK some school years were allowed to return before others in the summer term of 2020, and children around the world faced disruption to their learning more acutely in certain school years.

Despite these differences, many siblings do grow up in socially similar times and eras, and this generational proximity means that key life course transitions – such as those age-bound transitions surrounding education, including starting compulsory education, moving to secondary school, taking examinations and so on – as well as other transitions less directly defined by age – such as getting married, buying a home, having children, retiring and so on – are often experienced in tandem or close succession. Ideas about the ways in which the temporality of the life course is experienced are also explored by Jenny Hockey and Allison James (2003) who, following Edmund Leach (1966), consider how we can experience growing older when the gradual passing of time cannot be perceived through the senses. Hockey and James use anthropological accounts of rites of passage to suggest that such moments may enable us to experience time passing through acts of repetition, change and transformation. Our relationships are central to our expectations and experiences of these rites of passage, yet the idea that our lives are linked to those of others is largely absent from literature exploring the life course (May, 2019). Siblings are particularly pertinent here. In addition to their generational proximity, characteristics of siblingship outlined in previous chapters such as normative expectations surrounding age and birth-order roles, the changing complexities of care and closeness, the enhanced ways of 'knowing' that come from growing up together, and the challenges of being constructed as one in a series, all mean that being and having siblings can have a profound effect on the way the life course is experienced. Growing up with siblings can enhance our ability to experience and know the passage of time, intensifying the temporal markers of rites of passage.

These rites of passage are also governed by cultural norms. May discusses the role of 'temporal scripts' which 'set out *social norms* that delineate how we "should" grow up and grow older' (2019: 87, original emphasis). These cultural narratives about the life course comprise 'prescribed timetables that provide a road map for what kinds of things should happen at what points in life' (May, 2019: 89). Kineret Lahad (2017) similarly points to temporal norms in her analysis of the gendered construction of singlehood, where older single women disrupt norms around age and marriage. A straight-forward analysis of clock time can miss the rich ways in which our personal lives are temporally situated. May argues: 'Examining adulthood from a sociology of personal life angle shows the variety of social clocks regarding relationships, education and work, among other things, that adults are embedded in and expected to adhere to throughout their lives' (2019: 95).

I think that siblings are a particularly useful angle from which to explore time and the life course – the waxing and waning of age gaps and birth order reveals how biological time is constructed and lived within relationships, and the way in which siblings can provide a foil or accounting tool to one another when navigating key life course moments and milestones reveals the relational nature of these too. We saw this in the discussion of the relational construction of identity between sisters Anna and Francesca in Chapter 2.

In her study of sister relationships, Melanie Mauthner points to similarly temporally situated relationalities through the stories of sisters Zoe and Sofia, where Zoe's experiences of education are used to help guide her younger sister Sofia through the education system, helping her to avoid repeating the same mistakes. Zoe describes her feelings on finding out that Sofia 'bunked off' school (truanted) as she herself had done many times: 'I was angry, I was like, goddam you! I've done it... I've messed up badly, I don't want you messing up as well' (quoted in Mauthner, 2005b: 36). Despite her adopting this older, wiser sister role, Mauthner also includes quotes from Zoe in which she describes how she gains from her relationship with Sofia, telling her about her life in college and valuing her 'second person opinion' (quoted in Mauthner, 2005b: 36). Being only one year apart in age, Zoe and Sofia are navigating education in close enough succession to be able to learn from and help one another.

Thus we see that focusing on sibling relationships can help reveal some of the relational ways that time and the life course can be experienced. Focusing on youth transitions to adulthood, Ulrich Beck (1992) identified a shift from what he terms 'normal' biographies based around predetermined normative life plans and roles to 'choice' biographies characterised by individual responsibility and choice in transitions to adulthood. For Beck, these changes have brought about a new set of unequally distributed risks and uncertainties in late modernity which must be negotiated in day-to-day life, including increased fragmentation and unpredictability in what were once familiar and inevitable pathways to adulthood. But even in the absence of parentally provided 'route maps' to adulthood (Furlong and Cartmel, 2007), critiques of theories of individualisation and de-traditionalisation emphasise how we still progress through life as relational beings (Mason, 2004), and we saw in Mauthner's account of Zoe's discussion of her relationship with Sofia that they are navigating their path through education together. Indeed, a focus on the loss of 'normal' biographies and lack of route maps implicitly assumes that only intergenerational ties with parents are of use in assisting young people in their transitions to adulthood, overlooking the often significant influence of siblings.

Even when siblings do not attend the same school at the same time, their sibling relationships can carry over into school through their knowledge of a sibling's experience. Indeed, growing up in the same familial generation, often in the same household, can make siblings a foil – a comparison and accounting tool – for young people when considering their progress at school, and watching an older sibling advance though the education system can provide a unique insight into a young person's own educational journey. In the following example from my own interviews with young people, Farhana (age 14, British Pakistani Muslim, interviewed at Highfields) is describing how she quite literally provided a route map for her little sister so that she wouldn't get lost in the school building on her first day of secondary school. Farhana reflected on her own experience of getting lost, discussing why she had done this for her sister:

> Farhana: Erm, it was quite funny like at first cos she was really scared I was like, 'There's nothing to be scared about all the teachers are really nice' so it's quite good and well you know once you get used to the environment it's fine, you know.
>
> Interviewer: Yeah, it's quite a big shock isn't it from primary school?
>
> Farhana: It is isn't it, it's really big and I think the workload is quite dramatic. I think on my first day I got lost and even though I asked for instructions I still got lost … I gave my little sister a mini tour of the school before she came so yeah, so hopefully she didn't get lost, she didn't – thank God – unlike me. [laughs] So yeah, erm, I think you could also you know like tell them [younger siblings] which teachers to be aware of, er, things like that … And I think, erm, the workload you can, I think you can, erm, ask them for a lot of advice, erm, cos in some of my work I sometimes I don't quite understand it when I'm at home I would remember at school and then when I come home I just forget and I blank out. So yeah, I would ask my erm, elder sister. So yeah, my little sister goes that with me so it's good.

Here Farhana is drawing on her own past experiences to help her younger sister navigate the transition to secondary school. Their generational proximity means they are both navigating the same school corridors, but the fact that Farhana went first means her little sister is not finding her way as an atomised individual – she literally has a map. Watching an older sibling progress through the education system can have a significant impact on how young people conceptualise themselves at school. Observing an older sibling as they face important moments, make choices and progress through education enabled many young people I interviewed to better imagine what experiences such as attending university might be like for them. The proximity offered by growing up together, often in the same house, and the day-to-day nature of the observations and conversations this facilitates mean that knowledge of a sibling's experience can 'soak in' over time. Even young participants in the study who had not directly asked their older siblings for advice had a clear sense of what they thought things had been like for them. These impressions are constructed relationally within the context of the family, and we saw some of the dynamics of this in Chapter

2 in the discussion of how scripts around sibling identities are constructed. This is evident in the following focus group discussion (among 13–14-year-olds at Highfields school) about how knowledge about the significance of certain school years is accrued:

> Maleehah: I think you get sense in Year 9 cos your parents talk to ya a lot and say that 'look you've got your GCSEs' and your brothers and sisters talk to you and you've got your GCSEs, you've got two years left...
>
> Reece: [overlapping] My parents will talk to me but I just, I make it myself.
>
> Ryan: [overlapping] I'm trying my best to learn these next two years.
>
> Maleehah: [overlapping] I think if you've got older mates then that'd help. I've got older mates, I've got a lot of older mates and that helps a lot cos they're like 'ah look'. Cos I've got one mate that like, she got kicked out for having a little fight but she regrets it now she's in college, she regrets it now and she always like gives me a lecture...
>
> Tom: My sister, now she's doing her GCSEs she's gotta do so much revising and writing and stuff and I I've realised now that I'm gonna have to do that so I better just...
>
> Ryan: Get you head down.
>
> Tom: Yeah.
>
> Maleehah: That's just sick to watch...
>
> ...
>
> Ryan: My brother keeps telling me about it. He's 25 this year and he just keeps going on 'You've gotta try hard or you're gonna end up doing nothing in life.' He does it all the time.

In this discussion, we see how young people have received advice from older peers and siblings. Rachel Brooks (2007) writes about the role that peers can play in young people's decision making about education, and here we see the role of older peers in Maleehah's thinking. However, siblings are often even more useful than peers in helping young people orientate themselves towards education. For one thing, older siblings are often a broker in accessing networks of older peers, and the day-to-day knowledge of siblings' lives that can be acquired when siblings live together means that an understanding of the realities of studying for GCSE exams can be accrued through observation alone.

In the following focus group discussion, young people (ages 13–14, at Highfields school) are reflecting on how watching the experiences of their older siblings has helped them to make decisions about their next steps after secondary education and whether they will stay on at their school's sixth form college to take A levels:

Paul: My sisters did it so they stayed on and they seemed to enjoy it so...

Yasmin: I always wanted to be rich [laughs]

...

Interviewer: So do you think it helps if you've got older brothers and sisters who have gone before you and you know their choices?

Yeah.

Lyndsay: Cos they know what it's like and they give advice you know cos they've done it?

Yeah

Yeah

Kaseem: Yeah, cos like one of my brothers went to college and now he's in university and my other one didn't go college and he said he wish he did.

...

Yasmin: Well, yeah, because erm my big brother's gone to college and it sounds all right so.

Older siblings did not have to be socially or academically 'successful' at school to be useful. Some young people explicitly reflected upon how observations of their older siblings' behaviour had motivated them to change their own attitude to schooling so as to secure a different outcome for themselves. These young people were often able to piece together their knowledge of their sibling's school career at various points, identifying causal factors for their sibling's perceived level of success or failure. Take the following comment by 12-year-old

Aiden about his older sister and how his perceptions of her struggles with studying and the subsequent pay-off from her hard work have affected the way he approaches his own school work: 'When she was trying to get into university, I know how hard it is cos she was getting annoyed and then the work paid off. So I'll be like, "Yeah, I'm doing a lot of work. I don't like it, but it might pay off for me."'

Cameron Simmonds (a 14-year-old white British pupil at Highfields) also considered his own actions at school in light of the trajectories of his older brothers, both of whom were said by teachers to have succumbed to what they termed 'The Simmonds' Downfall at Year 9'. The teachers' assumption was that Cameron would follow the same trajectory and start to flounder when he reached Year 9 (the third year of secondary education in the UK). Cameron interpreted the narrative of 'The Simmonds' Downfall' as an incentive to act differently and break the pattern, stating, 'I just wanted to prove 'em wrong.' The way Cameron discussed his observations of the outcome of his brothers' school experiences, relating this to his own attempts to secure a different outcome for himself, indicates his longitudinal vantage point as a younger sibling and the relational way he makes sense of his own school self:

> My oldest brother was a lot like me; he did his work, he just proper got along with his work and then about Year 9 he started mixing with the wrong crowd, like I haven't done, and he started going off his work and just messing about ... He missed, like the first two years of college because he was working and was a mess ... He messed up pretty much but then now he's back on track, he's got a part-time job and he's at college ... But my other brother, he's got an apprentice-ship. He got, he did pretty much exactly the same as him ... but he hasn't decided to go to college.

The formation of this narrative is significant. Although Cameron tells the story in chronological order, starting with how his brothers behaved in their early secondary school years, explaining what happened in Year 9 and concluding with the outcome of the story (what they are doing now), it is likely that he has pieced the account together in hindsight, with his memories of what his brothers were like at school formed through narratives created by his teachers and parents. This is alluded to below as Cameron uses his structural position as the youngest sibling, and particularly his distance from his brothers in age, to make sense of why he has been able to avoid succumbing to 'The Simmonds' Downfall':

> I think it's the middle one kinda copies the older one cos they're pretty close ages, they're kind of, they're practically the same year, they go through the same stuff. But me, cos I didn't really go to school with either of them … I didn't copy anything they did, I didn't know what they got up to at school. I knew to an extent what they got up to in school but other than that I didn't know so I was totally different because I never got to see what they were like. And I didn't wanna know what they were like.

Although here Cameron is explaining that he is different from his brothers because he did not know much about their school selves, it is clear from the earlier extract that in fact he is also different because he *does* know, and his knowledge is of a narrative of how failure occurs which Cameron uses as a foil now.

Most younger siblings in the sample spoke of imagining their future in relation to an older sibling in terms of wishing to replicate success. Some, however, like Cameron, talked more in terms of learning from mistakes. Thus, through their position as the youngest sibling, young people are sometimes able to use the hindsight acquired vicariously through piecing together the causes of older siblings' educational outcomes in order to gain foresight (an ability to predict their own future trajectory and alter their behaviour accordingly).

This acquisition of both hindsight and foresight is brought about by the temporal and domestic proximities experienced by many siblings who grow up together in the same household and can help younger siblings to orientate themselves successfully towards their future educational transitions and perform well in the classroom. Older siblings can provide a route map to adulthood, acting as a guide for younger siblings in identifying and negotiating phases of their educational careers, and this route map can be accessed by younger siblings vicariously, regardless of the 'quality' of the relation-ship or the intentions of their older sibling. Furthermore, the influence of Cameron's significantly older brothers demonstrates the lasting stickiness of siblingship in the context of education. Of course, it is also possible for older siblings to gain foresight and hindsight from younger siblings who, for example, might inspire them to apply to or critique the value of university, or resit exams (Heath,

Fuller and Johnston 2010). Crucially, siblings are not just another form of influence to be considered alongside that of friends or family more generally, but rather they offer a particular temporal and domestic proximity which 'sticks' with young people, even if they do not physically attend the same school at the same time.

As discussed earlier in this chapter, generational proximity does not always mean that siblings experience the same environment. Family relationships and practices are also constantly shifting and can go through periods of rapid change or upheaval. Although we might be able to identify similarities between the experiences of siblings raised in the same home by the same parents, we cannot assume that their experiences and opportunities are the same. Siblings can also experience different configurations or 'eras' of the family unit according to their age, so younger siblings who are still at home when their parents divorce or encounter a change in financial cir-cumstances, for example, are brought up in a very different environ-ment from older siblings who may have left home by this stage. Young people I spoke to were very aware of the impact of such different family eras and environments, and were reflective about the effect of this on themselves, perhaps more so than sociologists at times. For example, in the quote below 13-year-old Caitlin from Highfields is thinking about why her younger sister is very sporty while she has no interest in sport. In doing so, she reflects specifically on the significance of the difference in age between herself and her sister when their step-father joined the family:

> I don't know [why her sister likes sport and she does not], I think because when my mum met my stepdad she [her sister] was only 3 and he was really into sport and stuff and when we were younger we used to like go out and play football and stuff, but I never liked it but she really liked it and stuff. So I think that's why, but because my mum's not sporty at all. I'm just like my mum.

Thus, Caitlin's step-father is understood as having a greater influence on her sister because of her relatively young age when he joined the family compared to Caitlin.

F4873, a mass observer whose gender and age are not known but who has two older sisters and one older brother, also identified how their older sisters grew up in a different era to them and their brother. The observer reflects on how their parents' approach to discipline changed alongside wider cultural shifts, with the author and their brother benefiting from what they see as a 'more liberal era' than their sisters, who were 'indoctrinated' by their parents' particular view of life. Jennifer Mason and Stewart Muir describe how family time can be 'bundled' together into eras which are 'packages of generalized "time out of time"' and part of 'how memories are "indexed" in and through time' (2013: 607). So we can see that Caitlin might bundle the time after her step-father joined her family as an era, or mass observer F4873 might consider the time before their parents relaxed their discipline a little as an era in their memories of family time.

Birth order and age gap

In the final section of this chapter I turn to look in more detail at issues of age in sibling relationships. The transitions to adulthood described in the previous section closely pertain to biological age, as the significance of birth order and age gap are heightened when navigating age-related institutions such as school. Other key moments in the life course, such as getting married or having children, are also governed by normative temporal scripts concerning age as well as gender (Lahad, 2017). However, we have also seen that age and birth order are not static, and the accounts of the shifts in sibling relationships through the life course outlined earlier in this chapter have indicated how birth order and age gap can be less keenly felt as people progress through the life course. This is also culturally specific. In her account of kinship among Pakistani families in England, Alison Shaw, for example, highlights the enhanced role of the older brother in many UK Pakistani families, particularly in terms of making decisions on behalf of younger siblings. Shaw writes that, though there are inevitable tensions, 'The fact that within the family each member has a clearly defined role according to age and sex means that there is relatively limited scope for following individual inclinations and initiatives' (2000: 94). In this sense, sibling age can straddle both 'natural' and 'social' interpretations of calendar time. Barbara Adam (1990; 2004) criticises binary debates about time as either natural or social, arguing that this dichotomy obscures the idea that time is both fundamentally natural – in the sense that we are part of the natural world – and social – in the sense that ideas of 'natural' time are socially produced. Looking at sibling relationships helps to reveal the interaction between natural and social time in the shifting significance of age and birth order through the life course, where biological age can be important due to more 'natural' factors such as size differences or cognitive development, as well as being important due to 'socially constructed' factors such as school year or becoming a legal adult. Similarly, biological age can itself be disrupted by shifts in the sibling relationship over time and the differently felt influence of other sociocultural factors.

Indeed, there are many examples from mass observers' accounts of observers reflecting on the changing meanings of birth order and age gap (we saw this with the example at the beginning of this chapter, where the age gap between the mass observer and her younger sister became less important following the 1920s party). Other mass observers wrote about age gaps becoming almost irrelevant as they got older. In her analysis of change and continuity in family life, Dorothy Jerrome suggests that siblings' shared pasts give them 'symbolic significance' (1994: 21) and draws on anthropological work on age-grade systems to consider how siblings may at times belong to the same 'grade', producing 'a sense of "shared" time and relative distance from people in other grades' (1994: 22). Jerrome discusses how the older sibling must eventually move on to the next grade, leaving their younger brothers and sisters behind, though we have perhaps seen a more complex picture that does not necessarily follow a linear progression through the life course. For some, a close age gap meant that shared cultural reference points provided shared memories of films, toys and games enjoyed as children. As the following observer (E5040) states about him and his sister:

> We have many common experiences and reference points, because we were close in age, and this means that as we get older we recall these with some amusement, and in some ways it brings us closer, even though we may not have seen each other for a while.

Ultimately there is no magic formula for working out how age gaps can affect a sibling relationship and age can vary in importance and change over time. While age often seems to feel more fixed in childhood, it is still negotiated within childhood relationships (Punch, 2005) and can be resisted. In the following quote from an interview with Craig (a 14-year-old boy interviewed in the estate youth club), he resists his younger calendar age, claiming that this is not what matters when considering the age gap between himself and his older sister. Here being 'old in the head' is more significant than biological or calendar age: 'Cos I reckon, er, I'm mature enough. I reckon, like, I'm really old in the head me. Like … my sister, I don't reckon she's as old in the head as me.'

Conclusion

In this chapter I have explored the temporal dimensions of siblingship, demonstrating how sibling relationships may change over time, with the significance of birth order and age gap shifting through the life course. Siblingship is imbued with temporality, from the everyday knowing that comes with growing up in close proximity to the ways that siblings may experience generational proximity or different socio-economic or family 'eras'. Growing up and ageing with siblings also means that certain life course events, such as educational transitions or the ageing of one's parents, can be experienced as part of a 'temporal convoy' (Gillis, 1997). Thus, accounting for the role of time in shaping sibling relationships is important, particularly as most sociological accounts of siblingship focus on childhood.

Exploring the temporalities of siblingship as we age also encourages us to notice the relational and social aspects of time. Thinking with siblings exposes the social construction of biological age, and we see how age and birth order can be more or less important at different points in the life course. We also see how aspects of the life course are experienced relationally as siblings might compare their experiences, provide one another with route maps to navigate more structural pathways (such as those through the education system) and provide support at key moments, for example during illness or when facing the end of a parent's life. Furthermore, looking at the temporal dynamics of siblingship can help bring together different aspects of sociological approaches to time so we are able to see how memory, generation and youth transitions interact with normative ideas of age in the way people's sibling relationships are lived.

Conclusion

A sociology of siblings

This book has explained why siblings matter. Siblings are a significant part of many people's lives, but, despite a growing body of empirical work exploring people's experiences of sibling relationships, questions about siblingship have remained on the periphery of sociological thought. By drawing on theories of relationality (Mason, 2004; Smart, 2007; Roseneil and Ketokivi, 2006), this book has demonstrated the sociological importance of sibling ties. These theoretical frames have helped to situate the meaning of sibling relationships in terms of how they are practised, their influence on decision making and on the relational construction of the self, as well as illuminating how sibling relationships ebb and flow through the life course as among our longest-lasting relationships. By thinking about siblings in terms of relationality – as a relationship in which we are deeply embedded and which, in turn, is tangled in webs of relationships with others – it is possible to see how siblingship continues to matter, even if it is a negative or destructive relationship. Similarly, the book has illuminated the significance of siblings even if they are absent altogether or exist only in the realm of an imagined relationship that might have been. In demonstrating the importance of siblings, this book has indicated that more sociological attention needs to be paid to this subject, not just as a relational form worthy of study within the field of family sociology, but also in the application of broader sociological themes such as the self, understandings of love, care and the meanings of relatedness, normativity and imagination and age, generation and life course.

Chapter 1 indicated the sorts of empirical and theoretical questions that scholars have posed about siblings, highlighting the need for more sociologically informed questions that are able to account for the diverse ways in which sibling relationships are practised and experienced. The chapters that followed extended the sociology of siblings, taking this work in new directions, exploring how the study of siblings can offer different framings of familiar sociological fields as well as opening up new agendas of sociological inquiry. The book probed how key sociological concepts can help foster a sociology of siblings capable of explaining why these relationships matter. By thinking sociologically, the book has revealed the profound influence of siblings, focusing on four key tenets of sociological thought: self, relationality, imagination and time (which are interwoven in the discussion with other elements such as gender, class, education, space and place) to unpack how siblings influence our lives. In so doing, the book has drawn on a diverse range of sociological litera-tures including theories of the relational self, identity, social care, kinship, embodied and sensory relationalities, ethereality, normativity, generation, age and life course, putting these sociological ideas to work to craft a sociology of siblingship.

This book has demonstrated that siblings influence our sense of who we are and who we can become in the future. Building on a case study of two young sisters' accounts of their lives at school and home, and their sense of who they are and who they might become in the future, Chapter 2 illustrated the importance of sibling relationships to the construction of the self. The chapter showed how identity is constructed in relation to the sibship, or sibling group, as a whole, due to practices of comparing siblings and preoc-cupations with similarities and differences between siblings. The chapter examined how the particularities of sibling relationships – such as presumed shared genetic relatedness and upbringing and the fascination associated with figuring out the mysteries of resem-blance between siblings – lend themselves to this comparing, with siblings occupying the role of a particularly significant 'other' in these processes. In so doing, the chapter pointed to the relational politics and interpersonal power dimensions in which stories of similarity and difference are told and retold, exploring how reputation transfers or 'rubs off' between siblings in different contexts, such as school and community, and explaining how this is enhanced by the 'evidential' relatedness of resemblances (Mason, 2008). In these discussions, the chapter unpacked the paradox of being one in a series of siblings in the context of a Western emphasis on the free-thinking autonomous self, who must plough their own furrow in life (Taylor, 1991; Rose, 1996). Ultimately, this chapter indicated the centrality of siblings to the formation of the self, not just as one of a list of important influences, but because the mystery of siblingship – the conundrums around how and why siblings may turn out to be similar to or different from one another – and how this is lived in different contexts means that siblings influence the formation of the self in particular and profound ways that ought to be part of our sociological analyses.

The complexities, ambivalences and apparent contradictions inherent to many sibling relationships, as well as the embodied, sensory and sometimes otherworldly or uncanny connections between siblings, mean that siblings are more than just an often overlooked category of relationship. Chapter 3 outlined the experiences and meanings of siblingship in people's lives, demonstrating how siblings may care for each other in different contexts, emphasising the significance of a background sort of 'being there' (Brownlie, 2014) among siblings and unpicking some of the different ways that sibling-ship is done (Morgan, 1996; 2011) in various settings such as home, school, holiday club and in the local community. Furthermore, the chapter emphasised the embodied closeness that can characterise sibling relationships, especially in childhood, as a relational form particularly imbued with sensations (H. Davies, 2015; Mason, 2018). In exploring what it means to be a sibling, the chapter also pointed to less tangible, more ethereal or uncanny connections between siblings whose relationship might be characterised by a certain 'ineffable kinship' (Mason, 2018). In short, this chapter demonstrated how siblings are not only a significant relational form that warrants further investigation, but a tie that can epitomise some of the meanings of relationality itself.

Chapter 4 was premised on the idea that not only do we live with our siblings, but we also live with the *idea* of siblings. The chapter highlighted the interplay between normative ideals of sibling-ship that might comprise scripts about idealised age and gender roles, and the complexities and messiness of experiences of sibling relationships as they are lived. The chapter developed John Gillis's

(1997) notion of a disconnect between the idealised families we live by and the realities of the families we live with, in relation to the particularities and complexities of sibling relationships as highlighted in Chapter 3. The chapter also emphasised how normative scripts pertaining to how siblingship ought to be experienced interact with imagined or yearned-for sibling relationships. Ultimately the chapter argued that part of what makes siblings so important is the role that ideas about siblings have in our life. In so doing, the chapter concluded with a detailed analysis of how understandings of kinship and everyday lay expertise about how things are passed on in families (Edwards, 2000) implicate siblingship in how we 'turn out'. Again, it is the particularities of siblingship – the intriguing questions of birth order and of 'nature versus nurture' – that render these normative understandings so potent.

Being and having siblings implicates our experiences of various facets of temporality. Chapter 5 began with a mass observer's account of her sibling relationships narrated as a kind of life story told though and with siblingship. By unpacking the temporal themes that this account generates, from the shifting quality and experience of sibling relationships over time to the role of memories and critical moments of 'transition', the story set up the discussion of the importance of bringing sibling relationships into conversation with sociological accounts of time. The chapter picked up on discussions of 'being there' (Brownlie, 2014) from Chapter 4 and examined how the background presence of siblings, coupled with the longevity of the tie, can render siblings 'temporal convoys' (Gillis, 1997) though the life course. The chapter also unpacked the importance of generational proximity in the potential for siblings to influence us at key moments in the life course. Dismantling some of the taken-for-granted assumptions about siblingship – for example, regarding the importance of birth order as a fixed category – the chapter pointed to how birth order and age gaps can wax and wane at different points in time, as their significance can come into sharp focus or seem to lessen in importance in various contexts and life course 'stages'. Troubling assumptions of siblingship as a straight-forwardly lateral tie, the chapter also illustrated how even siblings who are close in age may experience different sociocultural, economic or familial 'eras' with the potential to impact how they turn out in life. Thus, the chapter demonstrated the importance of paying attention to the various temporal facets of sibling relationships which are tangled together in siblings' lives.

Turning out as a sibling

The idea that siblings affect how we turn out is an ongoing theme which runs throughout this book. While working with the data and thinking about the significance and influence of siblingship, I have found myself often returning to the phrase 'turning out' to explain a sense of personhood, of the development of character, skills, personality and attributes through time which cannot quite be captured with sociological concepts such as 'self', 'transition' or 'educational achievement'. The chapters of this book have demonstrated that siblings are a key influence in how we turn out, from imparting an important, generationally proximate source of knowledge about key institutions such as education, to providing a complex and often contradictory sense of closeness, care and connection in addition to siblings' implication in the relational construction of identity. The idea of siblings and how they ought to behave, how siblings ought to treat one another, and how being and having siblings ought to be experienced influences our (gendered and aged) sense of whether we are turning out to be a 'good' big brother, younger sister and so on. Of course, the longevity of many sibling relationships and their role as 'temporal convoys' (Gillis, 1997) also means that they continue to affect us and remain a source of comparison throughout the life course. Though the process of turning out will never be completed, there is a sense that, as time passes, we may gain more insight into what a 'turned-out' person might look like – which elements of our selves feel established, decided or fixed in some way by our decisions, circumstances or luck – and we saw this in many of the mass observers' descriptions of themselves and their siblings through middle age and beyond, in which some expressed surprise or sadness at how their sibling's life had progressed in terms of health, relationships or jobs, for example. This was also present in young people's narratives and, despite their relatively early position in the life course, there was often a certain sense of fixity to accounts of being the 'good' or 'clever' sibling, even though we understand sociologically that the 'project of the self' is never finished, even after death (Jenkins, 2004), and constitutes a performance, endlessly adapted according to different contexts and audiences (Goffman, 1959).

The lay idea of turning out is useful, though, because it brings together many of the aspects of siblingship that have been discussed in this book, such as self, identity, labelling, issues of nature versus nurture, imagination and time in a manner that does not separate these into distinct analytical categories. For example, the discussions in this book have indicated that the construction of identity in relation to one's siblings is implicated by the labelling of others, the discursive tropes about sibling roles and the nature of relatedness between siblings in the popular imagination, in addition to family resemblances and the mysteries of nature versus nurture, which themselves ebb and flow over time and through the life course. The lay term 'turning out' is useful in that it does not reduce the tangling of these different concepts and categories of analysis to one sociological term or idea. Taken together, the ideas in this book demonstrate that siblings matter in profound ways because they influence how we turn out; how we think about ourselves in the past and present as well as how we imagine our future selves, the decisions we make, the ways we make sense of what it means to be human and what we are made up of. We see these factors play out in the public fascination with siblingship that was outlined in the introduction, and we see them reflected in some of the statistical hypotheses that scholars have used in their attempts to crack open the mysteries of birth order, sibship size, age group or gender configuration discussed in Chapter 1. However, we do not see many sociological questions regarding 'turning out' as a sibling, and this book seeks to begin these important conversations.

Power and diversity in sibling relationships

In starting a conversation about turning out as a sibling, this book has inevitably highlighted areas that require further study and has been focused mainly on siblingship as it is experienced in the minority world. Attempts have been made here to consider other contexts. For example, China's one-child policy, which ended in 2015, was discussed in relation to assumptions about the effect of being and having no siblings on how children will turn out, and Mary Chamberlain's (2006) account of siblingship in both Caribbean and UK contexts was utilised when considering the meanings of siblingship and the creation of sibling-like relationships. Miri Song's (1997; 2010) work on mixed-race siblings remains of crucial importance, particularly given the rise in mixed-race/heritage people in the UK (accounting for 2.2% of the population of England and Wales in the 2021 Census). However, more work needs to be done to explore questions of turning out as a sibling in global contexts in the majority world. For example, are any elements of the intriguing nature of siblings depicted in this book also present in other contexts? Do siblings fascinate in the same ways as an example of nature versus nurture, or are different frames significant outside of Western preoccupations? Do sibling practices of emotion and care differ and how is birth order and age experienced in other parts of the world? It is likely that some of the complexities of the interactions between being a sibling and Western ideals of the autonomous self that are outlined in this book are less relevant in other contexts, where assumptions and ideas about the self may take different forms. Loretta Baldassar and Rosa Brandhorst (2021) also point to the important role of sibling support across borders, and siblingship in transnational and migrant families is an important area that warrants further study.

Related to this is the question of ethnic diversity. I have drawn on the work of other scholars where possible throughout this book to think about how key themes such as responsibility, care, birth order, reputation and morality might be experienced differently by ethnic groups in the UK and beyond. I have particularly drawn on work by scholars such as Alison Shaw (2000) and Kalwant Bhopal (1997), who have written about some of the gendered practices particular to South Asian families. This has enabled me to consider how some of these themes may be lived and experienced within the gender dynamic of South Asian families. Miri Song's (2010) work has also highlighted the particular complexities of racism and colourism as experienced in mixed-race families. However, there remains a lack of work that looks particularly at sibling relationships in different ethnic contexts, and this is a space where more study is urgently needed. There is a role for both in-depth explorations and comparative work here in unpicking ethnic diversity in the ways siblings matter.

Of course, ethnic diversity also relates to power, and this is another area that would benefit from further study. Indeed, sibling relationships can feature serious abuses of power, and physical, emotional and sexual abuse between siblings remains an important but under-researched area. The less severe interpersonal power relationships between siblings that have featured in the accounts of sibling relationships in this book are interesting in that the generationally lateral nature of siblingship means siblings might be expected to have a more egalitarian relationship than other relational forms. For example, we have seen how parents and teachers have the power to create and reproduce narratives about similarities and differences between siblings. There are, however, points in the book where both young people and mass observers alluded to power dynamics between themselves and their siblings in terms of difficult behaviours, 'bossiness', differentials in physical power and inequalities in levels of responsibility. These dynamics appear to ebb and flow though the life course in a similar way to birth order and age, coming into sharper focus at certain points and lessening in importance at others.

Other issues of power and how they intersect with siblingship are also important and have not been explored fully here. Social class has remained on the periphery of the arguments laid out in this book, implicating discussions around sharing a home and the transference of reputation and siblingship in the local community, without benefiting from a detailed or sustained focus. Further study which focuses explicitly on class in shaping the experience of sibling relationships in the home, local community and at school is important. It would also be interesting to see how sibling relationships might be negotiated across growing differences in class identification, as siblings may find themselves in different economic positions or with different levels of education or types of employment as they age. We saw this to a certain extent in one mass observer's description of her anxieties about her future relationship with her sister in Chapter 5, where she worried that her changing financial position would create division and distance.

Issues of gender have also arisen throughout this book, particularly in the discussion of the heightened gendered roles and obligations that characterise the siblings we live by (Gillis, 1997) described in Chapter 4, and in terms of some of the embodied and relational sibling practices outlined in Chapter 3. However, more research is needed to explicitly unpack the gendered nature of sibling relationships and how they change over time, as well as how gender intersects with ethnicity in the construction and performance of sibling roles and relationships.

Researching siblings and siblingship

Researching sibling relationships and the meanings of siblingship presents methodological conundrums and opportunities. The data I have drawn upon in this volume focus primarily on individuals' reflections upon and narratives of their sibling relationships. This has enabled an emphasis on the effect of siblingship (including having no siblings) on people's lives. Inviting participants to reflect on their own sibling relationship(s) without fear that their sibling(s) might provide a counter-narrative also facilitated the incorporation of sibling relationships that are not positive. Indeed, this partiality has encouraged an analytical focus on stories of siblingship, and both mass observers' and young people's accounts were analysed narratively as well as thematically. This enabled an insight into how people make sense of the role of being and having siblings in their own life story, including reflections on the influence of siblings, similarities and differences between siblings, theories about how sibling relationships work and a sense of how siblings affect how people turn out in life.

The work of others has demonstrated the benefits of approaching the study of siblingship with the sibship (sibling group) as the unit of analysis, and studies such as those by Punch (2007), Mauthner (2005a; 2005b) and Song (2010) have fruitfully explored relational dynamics between siblings by interviewing siblings together and/or separately. Despite the focus on individual narrations, this book has also drawn upon serendipitous research opportunities to analyse sibship dynamics. Chapter 2, for example, began with an extended discussion of two interviews conducted with sisters Anna and Francesca. By conducting separate individual interviews I was able to compare their accounts in my analysis. This comparing was not aimed at somehow verifying the sisters' stories of their relationship, but rather enabled me to understand how the sisters' experiences and feelings about school, friendship and self were constructed in relation to one another. Chapter 3 included a discussion of my observation of siblings at a holiday club. These observations enabled an insight into embodied interactions between siblings and encouraged a focus on the ways siblingship is done in everyday settings. Furthermore, the theoretical framing of this book has pointed to the embedded nature of sibling relationships, which are lived and experienced as part of webs of relationships with others, and opportunities have been taken at points in the analysis to explicitly scrutinise this embeddedness. For example, in Chapter 2 the exploration of an interview with Mason and his mother enabled an analysis of the interpersonal politics and power relationships within which sibling identities are constructed. Similarly, the contextual nature of the interviews and focus groups with young people which were conducted in schools, youth clubs and homes highlight how sibling relationships are lived and experienced in different settings, and these particularities were explored in detail in Chapter 3.

Moving between different data sources has enabled this book to take the sociological analysis of siblingship in new directions. The use of focus groups with young people, for example, involving the discussion of a clip from the cartoon series *The Simpsons*, encouraged participants to take a stand and express an opinion about some of the more profound questions of siblingship which tap into wider normative ideals about sibling roles, as well as understandings about kinship and how things are 'passed on' in families. Conversely, the accounts of mass observers encourage a sense of biographical reflection in which, despite the variety in the types of responses to the directive on 'sibling relationships', there is a strong sense of writing for posterity in the written responses (Sheridan, 1993; Davies and Heaphy, 2011), engendering the narrating of sibling relationships through life stories, with emphasis placed on memory and life course.

In addition to offering insights capable of extending the sociology of siblings in new directions, this book has demonstrated the potential for siblings to be used as a lens to explore questions pertaining to the nature of the self, processes of socialisation and kinship. By asking people to reflect in abstract ways in response to vignettes about siblings as well as by encouraging them to reflect on their own sibling relationships and how they have shaped the ways they have 'turned out' in life, it is possible to access lay theories about the role of nature and nurture in these processes, with the sibling relationship becoming an elicitation tool for evoking reflections on these issues of selfhood and kinship.

Siblings and sociology

Using siblings as a methodological device, a key contribution of this book is rooted in its approach to thinking *with* as well as about siblings, identifying how siblings can be a useful lens through which to view other sociological themes, opening up our thoughts to different ways of looking, thinking and asking about social phenomena. Thinking with siblings brings new and exciting ways of approaching key issues of sociological significance and invites sociologists to pose different questions about the world.

First, this book has indicated how siblingship can help us to think differently about issues surrounding self and identity, both of which have been key anchor points in contemporary sociological theorising. By looking at how siblings influence the self, sociologists are encouraged to look horizontally as well as vertically for sources of influence, moving beyond the preoccupation with the effect of parents. This book has demonstrated how, as generationally proximate relationships, siblings offer a particular sort of social influence which can be explicit as well as implicitly 'soaked in' over years of 'being there' (Brownlie, 2014). The idea that siblings can be a test case for thinking about nature versus nurture also encourages the sociological imagination to stray into realms that may seem somewhat outside the sociological 'comfort zone', weaving ideas about physical appearance and genetic relatedness into our ideas about the formation of the relational self.

The book has also utilised siblings as a way to think about relationality. The chapters point to the complexities and ambivalences of sibling relationships, showing how they often comprise a combination of positive and negative emotions which can shift over time, and can include a background type of care as well as physical conflict. By using siblings to help us to think about relationality, it is possible to notice how care and connection as well as the experiences and feelings of relatedness can shift in different contexts. The particularly tumultuous nature of many people's sibling relationships, at least at some points in the life course, can also highlight the 'stickiness' (Smart, 2007; Davies, 2019) of sibling bonds that are so often characterised by a tangling of love, hate, conflict, care and ambivalence. Furthermore, by looking at the relational complexities of siblingship, the sociological gaze is drawn towards an understanding of the intertwining of areas of concern that might not traditionally be seen as belonging to sociological analyses of relationships. These include genetic connectedness (which seems to belong to science), sensorial connections (which seem to belong to the natural world) and ethereal connections (which can seem magical and otherworldly). Of course, all of these elements are sociological in that they inform our experience of society. While I do not claim to be the first to suggest that these facets of relationality that exist 'beyond' the social ought to be brought into sociological thought (see Mason, 2008; 2018; Nordqvist, 2010; H. Davies, 2015), I do think that siblings can be a useful lens for helping us to notice their interconnection with more traditionally sociological themes such as care and responsibility.

Expanding beyond relationality, the analysis presented in this book has used sibling relationships to scrutinise ideas about normativity and imagination in sociological thought. By looking at the interaction between normative ideas about how siblingship ought to be done and the complex lived realities of siblingship, the sociological gaze can be focused on the gaps between imagined ideals and everyday relationships. These gaps are where relationships are negotiated and made sense of and where the imaginary is woven together with lived experience in everyday life. Siblings are particularly useful here because these gaps between 'real life' and imagined sibling relationships are particularly large. The ups and downs of siblingship and the heightened embodied, spatial and generational proximities that characterise many children's sibling ties means that the lived experience of siblingship can be particularly messy. This messiness juxtaposes with normative scripts, not just about what an ideal sibling might be or do but also about how sibling relationships might affect how we turn out in life. Thus, looking at siblings encourages us to consider how normative ideas can affect our sense of how we make sense of our relationships, our everyday lives and our sense of who we are and who we can become. Thinking with siblings about these issues also points to the role of imagined or yearned-for relationships in the ways we consider and narrate our lives.

Finally, the book has used siblings as a lens through which to think about time. By looking at the different temporalities of sibling-ship and how they interconnect, this book has illuminated the social and relational construction of different facets of seemingly 'natural' or 'calendar' time. For example, calendar age, as it manifests in birth order or age gap between siblings, can become more or less important at different points in the life course, or siblings can feel as though they share a generation at some points in their life and then find themselves experiencing very different sociocultural or familial 'eras' (Mason and Muir, 2013) at other conjunctures. The analysis of time in this book has also responded to May's (2019) call for a relational approach to life course transitions, demonstrating how the particular comparability of siblingship, along with the ways many siblings grow up alongside one another, exposes how life course transitions are both imagined and experienced in relation to others. Ultimately, sibling relationships can encourage a recognition of the social and relational production of time in terms of age, life course transitions and generation, as well as how these temporalities interact with one another.

Running through these themes are questions of emotion, and the book has indicated how thinking with siblings can contribute to sociological understandings of emotions. The ups and downs of sibling relationships and the myriad of feelings that they cause – annoyance, love, security, care, jealousy, anger, hatred – demonstrate the temporally and contextually situated nature of emotion. Studying sibling relationships illuminates the ways that emotions are tangled with embodied and sensory affinities, and enacted through everyday practices as well as in imaginative realms.

Overall, this book has been something of a call to sociology to pay more attention to siblings. Siblings are full of interest because they tap into so many profound questions about who we are and who we can become, questions that are fundamental to the discipline of sociology. The cultural fascination with siblingship is evident in countless fictional and non-fictional accounts, and siblings offer exciting possibilities for sociological thinking, both empirically and theoretically. Sociologists ought to be intrigued by siblings, as a relational form that matters, that can influence all aspects of life and that can help to illuminate different viewpoints on familiar themes, firing the sociological imagination and directing the analytical gaze.

References

Aaltonen, S. (2016), '"My mother thought upper secondary school was OK, but then my sibling said no" – Young People's Perceptions of the Involvement of Parents and Siblings in their Future Choices', *Sociological Research Online* 21.1: 65–76.

Adam, B. (1990), *Time and Social Theory*, Cambridge: Polity.

Adam, B. (2004), *Time* (Polity Key Concepts Series), Cambridge: Polity.

Bacon, K. (2012), '"Beings in their own right"? Exploring Children and Young People's Sibling and Twin Relationships in the Minority World', *Children's Geographies* 10.3: 307–19.

Baldassar, L., and Brandhorst, R. (2021), 'Sibling Support in Transnational Families: The Impact of Migration and Mobility on Sibling Relationships of Support Over Time and Distance', in A. Buchanan and A. Rotkirch (eds), *Brothers and Sisters Across the Life Course*, Basingstoke: Palgrave, 239–56.

Barabak, M. Z. (2015), 'Bush Brothers Have a Complex Relationship, Marked by Fierce Rivalry, Wounded Feelings', *The Los Angeles Times*, 17 June, https://www.latimes.com/nation/la-na-bush-brothers-20150617-story.html (accessed 1 August 2021).

Beck, U. (1992), *Risk Society: Towards a New Modernity*, London: Sage.

Bengtson, V. L., Biblarz, T. J., and Roberts, R. E. L. (2002), *How Families Still Matter: A Longitudinal Study of Youth in Two Generations*, Cambridge: Cambridge University Press.

Bennett, V. (2010), 'A Tale of Brotherly Love: When Siblings Fall Out, and Try to Make Up', *The Independent Online*, 26 September, http://www.vanorabennettauthor.com/?page_id=757 (accessed 10 September 2022).

Bhopal, K. (1997), 'South Asian Women within Households: Dowries, Degradation and Despair', *Women's Studies International Forum* 20.4: 483–92.

Blake, J. (1989), 'Number of Siblings and Educational Attainment', *Science (American Association for the Advancement of Science)* 245.4913: 32–6.

Bourdieu, P. (1990), *The Logic of Practice*, Cambridge: Polity.

Brooks, R. (2007), 'Friends, Peers and Higher Education', *British Journal of Sociology of Education* 28.6: 693–707.

Brownlie, J. (2014), *Ordinary Relationships: A Sociological Study of Emotions, Reflexivity and Culture*, Basingstoke: Palgrave Macmillan.

Burkitt, I. (2008), *Social Selves: Theories of Self and Society*, 2nd edn, London: Sage.

Carr Steelman, L., Powell, B., Werum, R., and Carter, S. (2002), 'Reconsidering the Effects of Sibling Configuration: Recent Advances and Challenges', *Annual Review of Sociology* 28: 243–69.

Carsten, J. (1997), *The Heat of the Hearth: The Process of Kinship in a Malay Fishing Community*, Oxford: Clarendon Press.

Carsten, J. (2000), '"Knowing where you've come from": Ruptures and Continuities of Time and Kinship in Narratives of Adoption Reunions', *The Journal of the Royal Anthropological Institute* 6.4: 687–703.

Carsten, J. (2004), *After Kinship*, Cambridge: Cambridge University Press.

Chamberlain, M. (1999), 'Brothers and Sisters, Uncles and Aunts: A Lateral Perspective on Caribbean Families', in E. B. Silva and C. Smart (eds), *The New Family?*, London: Sage, 129–42.

Chamberlain, M. (2006), *Family Love in the Diaspora: Migration and the Anglo-Caribbean Experience*, New Brunswick, NJ: Transaction.

Cicirelli, V. G. (1994), 'Sibling Relationships in Cross-Cultural Perspective', *Journal of Marriage and the Family* 56: 7–20.

Coleman, J. S. (1988), 'Social Capital and the Creation of Human Capital', *American Journal of Sociology* 94 Suppl.: S95–S120.

Coles, P. (2003), *The Importance of Sibling Relationships in Psychoanalysis*, London: Routledge.

Colt, R. M. (1993), 'Innocence Unleashed: The Power of the Single Child', in J. Stephens Mink and J. Doubler Ward (eds), *The Significance of Sibling Relationships in Literature*, Bowling Green, OH: Bowling Green State University Popular Press, 11–23.

Conley, D. (2004), *The Pecking Order: Which Siblings Succeed and Why*, New York: Pantheon.

Connor, S. (2013), 'One Child Policy: China's Army of Little Emperors', *The Independent*, 10 January, https://www.independent.co.uk/news/world/asia/one-child-policy-china-s-army-little-emperors-8446713.html (accessed 1 August 2021).

Dale, A., Fieldhouse, E., Shaheen, N., and Kalra, V. (2002), 'The Labour Market Prospects for Pakistani and Bangladeshi Women', *Work, Employment and Society* 16.1: 5–25.

Davidoff, L. (2012), *Thicker Than Water: Siblings and their Relations 1780–1920*, Oxford: Oxford University Press.

Davies, H. (2012), 'Affinities, Seeing and Feeling like Family: Exploring Why Children Value Face-to-face Contact', *Childhood* 19.1: 8–23.

Davies, H. (2015), *Understanding Children's Personal Lives and Relationships*, Basingstoke: Palgrave Macmillan.

Davies, K. (2015), 'Siblings, Stories and the Self: The Sociological Significance of Young People's Sibling Relationships', *Sociology* 49.4: 679–95.

Davies, K. (2019), '"Sticky" Proximities: Sibling Relationships and Education', *The Sociological Review* 67.1: 210–25.

Davies, K., and Heaphy, B. (2011), 'Interactions that Matter: Researching Critical Associations', *Methodological Innovation Online* 6.3: 5–16, https://journals.sagepub.com/doi/pdf/10.4256/mio.2011.002 (accessed 10 September 2022).

Davis, D. L. (2014), *Twins Talk: What Twins Tell us about Person, Self and Society*, Athens, OH: Ohio University Press.

Dunn, J. (1985), *Sisters and Brothers: The Developing Child*, Cambridge, MA: Harvard University Press.

Dunn, J. (2000 [1982]), 'State of the Art: Siblings', *The Psychologist* 13.5: 244–8.

Dunn, J., and Kendrick, C. (1982), *Siblings: Love, Envy and Understanding*, Cambridge, MA: Harvard University Press.

Edwards, J. (2000), *Born and Bred: Idioms of Kinship and New Reproductive Technologies in England*, Oxford: Oxford University Press.

Edwards, R., Hadfield, L., Lucey, H., and Mauthner, M. (2006), *Sibling Identity and Relationships: Sisters and Brothers*, Abingdon: Routledge.

Evans, R. (2011), '"We are managing our own lives ...": Life Transitions and Care in Sibling-headed Households Affected by AIDS in Tanzania and Uganda', *Area* 43.4: 384–96.

Faber, A., and Mazlish, E. (1998), *Siblings Without Rivalry: Helping your Children Live Together so You Can Live Too*, 2nd edn, London: Piccadilly Press.

Finch, J. (2007), 'Displaying Families', *Sociology* 41.1: 65–81.

Finch, J., and Mason, J. (1993), *Negotiating Family Responsibilities*, London: Routledge.

Finch, J., and Mason, J. (2000), *Passing On: Kinship and Inheritance in England*, London: Routledge.

Fong, V. L. (2004), *Only Hope: Coming of Age under China's One-child Policy*, Stanford, CA: Stanford University Press.

Franceschelli, M. (2016), *Identity and Upbringing in South Asian Muslim Families: Insights from Young People and their Parents in Britain*, Basingstoke: Palgrave Macmillan.

Franceschelli, M., and O'Brien, M. (2015), '"Being modern and modest": South Asian Young British Muslims Negotiating Multiple Influences on their Identity', *Ethnicities* 15.5: 696–714.

Franklin, S. (2003), 'Re-thinking Nature–Culture: Anthropology and the New Genetics', *Anthropological Theory* 3.1: 65–85.

Franklin, S., and Mckinnon, S. (eds) (2001), *Relative Values: Reconfiguring Kinship Studies*, Durham, NC: Duke University Press.

Furlong, A., and Cartmel, A. (2007), *Young People and Social Change: New Perspectives*, 2nd edn, Milton Keynes: Open University Press.

Giddens, A. (1991), *Modernity and Self Identity: Self and Society in the Late Modern Age*, Cambridge: Polity.

Giddens, A. (1992), *The Transformation of Intimacy: Sexuality, Love and Eroticism in Modern Societies*, Cambridge: Polity.

Gillies, V., and Lucey, H. (2006), '"It's a connection you can't get away from": Brothers, Sisters and Social Capital', *Journal of Youth Studies* 9.4: 479–93.

Gillis, J. R. (1997), *A World of Their Own Making: Myth, Ritual and the Quest for Family Values*, Cambridge, MA: Harvard University Press.

Goffman, E. (1959), *The Presentation of Self in Everyday Life*, London: Penguin.

Goffman, E. (1986 [1963]), *Stigma: Notes on the Management of a Spoiled Identity*, New York: Simon and Schuster.

Griffiths, G. (2020), 'Coronavirus: Is Lockdown Making Only Children Lonely?', BBC Online, 29 April, https://www.bbc.co.uk/news/uk-wales-52465054?intlink_from_url=& (accessed 1 September 2021).

Gubrium, J. F., and Holstein, J. A. (1998), 'Narrative Practice and the Coherence of Personal Stories', *The Sociological Quarterly* 39.1: 163–87.

Gubrium, J. F., and Holstein, J. A. (2009), *Analysing Narrative Reality*, London: Sage.

Gulløv, E., Palludan, C., and Wentzel Winther, I. (2015), 'Engaging Sibling-ships', *Childhood* 22.4: 506–19.

Haas, L. J. (2021), 'Jack, Bobby and Ted: The Untold Story of the Kennedy Brothers', *The Irish Times*, 9 April, https://www.irishtimes.com/culture/books/jack-bobby-and-ted-the-untold-story-of-the-kennedy-brothers-1.4524107 (accessed 1 September 2021).

Hadfield, L., Edwards, R., and Mauthner, M. (2006), 'Brothers and Sisters: A Source of Support for Children in School?', *Education* 34.1: 65–72.

Heaphy, B., and Davies, K. (2012), 'Critical Friendships', *Families, Relationships and Societies*, 1.3: 311–26.

Heath, S. (2018), 'Siblings, Fairness and Parental Support for Housing in the UK', *Housing Studies* 33.2: 284–98.

Heath, S., Fuller, A., and Johnston, B. (2010), 'Young People, Social Capital and Network-based Educational Decision-making', *British Journal of Sociology of Education* 31.4: 395–411.

Hegar, R. L. (2005), 'Sibling Placement in Foster Care and Adoption: An Overview of International Research', *Children and Youth Services Review* 27.7: 717–39.

Higgins, C. (2010), 'Romulus and Remus. Prospero and Antonio. David and Ed…', *The Guardian Online*, 27 September, https://www.theguardian.com/culture/charlottehigginsblog/2010/sep/27/edmiliband-davidmiliband#comment-7793723 (accessed 10 September 2022).

Hockey, J., and James, A. (2003), *Social Identities Across the Life Course*, Basingstoke: Palgrave Macmillan.

Hoffman, K. L., Kiecolt, K. J., and Edwards, J. N. (2005), 'Physical Violence Between Siblings A Theoretical and Empirical Analysis', *Journal of Family Issues* 26.8: 1103–30.

Holland, J. (2008), 'Young People and Social Capital: What Can it Do for Us', Families and Social Capital Research Group Working Paper No. 24, London South Bank University.

Holstein, J. A., and Gubrium, J. F. (2000), *The Self We Live By: Narrative Identity in a Postmodern World*, Oxford: Oxford University Press.

Howell, S., and Marre, D. (2006), 'To Kin a Transnationally Adopted Child in Norway and Spain: The Achievement of Resemblances and Belonging', *Ethnos* 71.3: 293–316.

Ince, C., Chappell, A., and McHugh, E. (2021), *Auto/Biographical Experiences of University Students from Military Families: The Same but Different*, London: Brunel University Press.

Jamieson, L. (1998), *Intimacy: Personal Relationships in Modern Societies*, Cambridge: Polity.

Jenkins, R. (2004), *Social Identity*, 2nd edn, London: Routledge.

Jerrome, D. (1994), 'Time, Change and Continuity in Family Life', *Ageing and Society* 14.1: 1–27.

Jones, C. (2016), 'Sibling Relationships in Adoptive and Fostering Families: A Review of the International Research Literature', *Children & Society* 30.4: 324–34.

Kettrey, H. H., and Emery, B. C. (2006), 'The Discourse of Sibling Violence', *Journal of Family Violence* 21.6: 407–16.

Kiselica, M. S., and Morrill-Richards, M. (2007), 'Sibling Maltreatment: The Forgotten Abuse', *Journal of Counseling and Development* 85.2: 148–60.

Kuo, H. D., and Hauser, R. M. (1997), 'How Does Size of Sibship Matter? Family Configuration and Family Effects on Educational Attainment', *Social Science Research* 26: 69–94.

Lacey, R. (2020), *Battle of Brothers: William and Harry, the Inside Story of a Family in Tumult*, London: Harper Collins.

Lahad, K. (2017), *A Table for One: A Critical Reading of Singlehood, Gender and Time*, Manchester: Manchester University Press.

Lahad, K., and May, V. (2021), 'Holding Back and Hidden Family Displays: Reflections on Aunthood as a Morally Charged Category', *Current Sociology* 69.7: 1002–17.

Lawler, S. (2008), *Identity: Sociological Perspectives*, Cambridge: Polity.

Leach, E. R. (1966), 'Two Essays concerning the Symbolic Representation of Time', in E. R. Leach, *Rethinking Anthropology*, London: Athlone, 124–36.

Levy, A. (1996), *Never Far from Nowhere*, London: Headline.

Liu, C., Munakata, T., and Onuoha, F. (2005), 'Mental Health Condition of the Only-child: A Study of Urban and Rural High School Students in China', *Adolescence* 40.160: 831–45.

Mannheim, K. (1952), *Essays on the Sociology of Knowledge*, London: Routledge.

Marre, D., and Bestard, J. (2009), 'The Family Body: Persons, Bodies and Resemblances', in J. Edwards and C. Salazar (eds), *European Kinship in the Age of Biotechnology*, New York: Berghahn Books, 64–78.

Mason, J. (2004), 'Personal Narratives, Relational Selves: Residential Histories in the Living and Telling', *Sociological Review* 52.2: 162–79.

Mason, J. (2008), 'Tangible Affinities and the Real Life Fascination of Kinship', *Sociology* 42.1: 29–45.

Mason, J. (2018), *Affinities: Potent Connections in Personal Life*, Cambridge: Polity.

Mason, J., and Davies, K. (2009), 'Coming to Our Senses? A Critical Approach to Sensory Methodology', *Qualitative Research* 9.5: 587–603.

Mason, J., and Muir, S. (2013), 'Conjuring up Traditions: Atmospheres, Eras and Family Christmases', *The Sociological Review* 61.3: 607–29.

Mason, J., and Tipper, B. (2008), 'Being Related: How Children Define and Create Kinship', *Childhood* 15.4: 441–60.

Mauthner, M. (2005a), 'Distant Lives, Still Voices: Sistering in Family Sociology', *Sociology* 39.4: 623–42.

Mauthner, M. (2005b), *Sistering: Power and Change in Female Relationships*, Basingstoke: Palgrave Macmillan.

May, V. (2018), 'Belonging across the Lifetime: Time and Self in Mass Observation Accounts', *The British Journal of Sociology* 69.2: 306–22.

May, V. (2019), 'Personal Life across the Lifecourse', in V. May and P. Nordqvist (eds), *The Sociology of Personal Life*, 2nd edn, Basingstoke: Palgrave, 87–100.

McCaffrey, M. (2008), 'Growing Up with a Disabled Sibling and Family Support: What Can be Done?', in M. Klett-Davis (ed.), *Putting Sibling Relationships on the Map: A Multi-Disciplinary Perspective*, London: The Family and Parenting Institute, 99–111.

McCormick, A. (2010), 'Siblings in Foster Care: An Overview of Research, Policy and Practice', *Journal of Public Child Welfare* 4: 198–218.

McIntosh, I., and Punch, S. (2009), '"Barter", "Deals", "Bribes" and "Threats"', *Childhood* 16.1: 49–65.

Mead, G. H. (1934), *Mind, Self, and Society*, Chicago: University of Chicago Press.

Mead, G. H. (1980 [1932]), *The Philosophy of the Present*, ed. A. E. Murphy, Chicago: University of Chicago Press.

Meakings, S., Coffey, A., and Shelton, K. A. (2017), 'The Influence of Adoption on Sibling Relationships: Experiences and Support Needs of Newly Formed Adoptive Families', *The British Journal of Social Work* 47.6: 1781–99.

Meltzer, A. (2018), 'Embodying and Enacting Disability as Siblings: Experiencing Disability in Relationships between Young Adult Siblings with and without Disabilities', *Disability & Society* 33.8: 1212–33.

Meyers, A. (2014), 'A Call to Child Welfare: Protect Children from Sibling Abuse', *Qualitative Social Work* 13.5: 654–70.

Meyers, A. (2017), 'Lifting the Veil: The Lived Experience of Sibling Abuse', *Qualitative Social Work: Research and Practice* 16.3: 333–50.

Misztal, B. A. (2003), *Theories of Social Remembering*, Milton Keynes: Open University Press.

Mitchell, J. (2003), *Siblings: Sex and Violence*, Cambridge: Polity.

Morgan, D. H. (1996), *Family Connections: An Introduction to Family Studies*, Cambridge: Polity.

Morgan, D. H. (2011), *Rethinking Family Practices*, Basingstoke: Palgrave Macmillan.

Nordqvist, P. (2010), 'Out of Sight, Out of Mind: Family Resemblances in Lesbian Donor Conception', *Sociology* 44.6: 1128–44.

Nordqvist, P. (2017), 'Genetic Thinking and Everyday Living: On Family Practices and Family Imaginaries', *The Sociological Review* 65.4: 865–81.

Parker, J., and Stimpson, J. (2002), *Raising Happy Brothers and Sisters: Helping our Children Enjoy Life Together, from Birth Onwards*, London: Hodder and Stoughton.

Powell, B., and Steelman, L. C. (1993), 'The Educational Benefits of Being Spaced Out: Sibship Density and Educational Progress', *American Sociological Review* 58.3: 367–81.

Powell, B., and Steelman, L. C. (1995), 'Feeling the Pinch: Child Spacing and Constraints on Parental Economic Investments in Children', *Social Forces* 73.4: 1465–86.

Prout, A., and James, A. (1997), 'A New Paradigm for the Sociology of Childhood? Provenance, Promise and Problems', in A. James and A. Prout (eds), *Constructing and Reconstructing Childhood: Contemporary*

Issues in the Sociological Study of Childhood, 2nd edn, London: Falmer, 7–32.

Punch, S. (2004), 'Negotiating Autonomy: Children's Use of Time and Space in Rural Bolivia', in V. Lewis, M. Kellett, C. Robinson, S. Fraser and S. S. Ding (eds), *The Reality of Research with Children and Young People*, London: Sage, 94–114.

Punch, S. (2005), 'The Generationing of Power: A Comparison of Child–Parent and Sibling Relations in Scotland', *Sociological Studies of Children and Youth* 10: 169–88.

Punch, S. (2007), '"I felt they were ganging up on me": Interviewing Siblings at Home', *Children's Geographies* 5.3: 219–34.

Punch, S. (2008), '"You can do nasty things to your brothers and sisters without a reason": Siblings' Backstage Behaviour', *Children & Society* 22: 333–44.

Rees, A., and Pithouse, A. (2019), 'Views from Birth Children: Exploring the Backstage World of Sibling Strangers', *Families, Relationships and Societies* 8.3: 361–77.

Ribbens McCarthy, J., Edwards, R., and Gillies, V. (2003), *Making Families: Moral Tales of Parenting and Step-parenting*, Durham: Sociology Press.

Richardson, S. L., and Jordan, S. L. (2017), 'Qualitative Inquiry of Sibling Relationships: Reinforcement of Disability Devaluation through the Exclusion of Voices', *Disability & Society* 32.10: 1534–54.

Rose, N. (1996), *Inventing Our Selves: Psychology, Power and Personhood*, Cambridge: Cambridge University Press.

Roseneil, S., and Ketokivi, K. (2006), 'Relational Persons and Relational Processes: Developing the Notion of Relationality for the Sociology of Personal Life', *Sociology* 50.1: 143–59.

Sanders, R. (2004), *Sibling Relationships: Theory and Issues for Practice*, Basingstoke: Palgrave Macmillan.

Saunders, H., and Selwyn, J. (2011), *Adopting Large Sibling Groups: The Experiences of Adopters and Adoption Agencies*, London: BAAF.

Sayer, A. (2011), *Why Things Matter to People: Social Science, Values and Ethical Life*, Cambridge: Cambridge University Press.

SCIE/NICE (Social Care Institute for Excellence/National Institute for Health and Care Excellence) (2010), 'SCIE/NICE Recommendations on Looked-after Children: Promoting the Quality of Life of Looked-after Children and Young People. Sibling Placements and Contact', www.scie.org.uk/publications/guides/guide40/recommendations/sibling.asp (accessed 22 August 2022).

Scott, S. (2018), 'A Sociology of Nothing: Understanding the Unmarked', *Sociology* 52.1: 3–19.

Scott, S. (2019), *The Sociology of Nothing: Silence, Invisibility and Emptiness in Social Life*, Abingdon: Routledge.

Segal, N. L. (1999), *Entwined Lives: Twins and What They Tell us about Human Behaviour*, New York: Plume.

Shaw, A. (2000), *Kinship and Continuity: Pakistani Families in Britain*, Amsterdam: Harwood Academic.

Sheridan, D. (1993), 'Writing to the Archive: Mass Observation as Autobiography', *Sociology* 27.1: 27–40.

Smart, C. (2007), *Personal Life: New Directions in Sociological Thinking*, Cambridge: Polity.

Smart, C., et al. (2012), 'Difficult Friendships and Ontological Insecurity', *The Sociological Review* 60.1: 91–109.

Song, M. (1997), '"You're becoming more and more English": Investigating Chinese Siblings' Cultural Identities', *New Community* 23.3: 343–62.

Song, M. (2010), 'Does "Race" Matter? A Study of "Mixed Race" Siblings' Identifications', *The Sociological Review* 58.2: 265–85.

Spencer, L., and Pahl, R. (2006), *Rethinking Friendship: Hidden Solidarities Today*, Princeton, NJ: Princeton University Press.

Stephens Mink, J., and Doubler Ward, J. (eds) (1993), *The Significance of Sibling Relationships in Literature*, Bowling Green, OH: Bowling Green State University Popular Press.

Stewart, E. A. (2000), *Exploring Twins: Towards a Social Analysis of Twinship*, Basingstoke: Palgrave.

Strathern, M. (1992), *After Nature: English Kinship in the Late Twentieth Century*, Cambridge: Cambridge University Press.

Taylor, C. (1991), *The Ethics of Authenticity*, Cambridge, MA: Harvard University Press.

Thompson, P. (1993), 'Family Myths, Models and Denials in the Shaping of Individual Life Paths', in D. Bertaux and P. Thompson (eds), *Between Generations*, London: Transaction Publishers, 13–38.

Toureille, C. (2021), 'Prince William's "Curt" Message to Prince Harry on his Birthday Showed their Relationship is still "Icy' and They Are no Closer to Making Up, Royal Expert Claims', *MailOnline*, 16 September, https://www.dailymail.co.uk/femail/article-9997079/Prince-William-Prince-Harry-not-ready-make-expert-claims.html (accessed 1 October 2021).

Towers, L. (2020), 'Life after Death: Experiences of Sibling Bereavement over the Life Course', unpublished PhD thesis, University of Sheffield.

Urry, J. (2002), 'Mobility and Proximity', *Sociology* 36.2: 255–74.

Wentzel Winther, I., Palludan, C., Gulløv, E., and Middelboe Rehder, M. (2015a), *Sibling: Practical and Sensitive Relations*, Copenhagen: Egmont Fonden, Aarhus University Press.

Wentzel Winther, I., Palludan, C., Gulløv, E., and Middelboe Rehder, M. (2015b), *(Ex)changeable Siblingship: Experienced and Practiced by Children and Young People in Denmark*, Copenhagen: Egmont Fonden, Aarhus University Press (film).

White, N., and Hughes, C. (2018), *Why Siblings Matter: The Role of Brother and Sister Relationships in Development and Wellbeing*, Abingdon: Routledge.

Index

9 781526 142177